M000209449

JOHN AND THE JOHANNINE LETTERS

General Editors
Core Biblical Studies
Louis Stulman, *Old Testament*
Warren Carter, *New Testament*

Other Books in the Core Biblical Studies Series
The Apocrypha by David A. deSilva
The Dead Sea Scrolls by Peter Flint
Apocalyptic Literature in the New Testament by Greg Carey
God in the New Testament by Warren Carter
Christology in the New Testament by David L. Bartlett
The Pentateuch by Marvin A. Sweeney

JOHN AND THE
JOHANNINE
LETTERS

COLLEEN M. CONWAY

Abingdon Press

Nashville

JOHN AND THE JOHANNINE LETTERS

Copyright © 2017 by Abingdon Press

All rights reserved.

No part of this work may be reproduced or transmitted in any form or by any means, electronic or me-chanical, including photocopying and recording, or by any information storage or retrieval system, except as may be expressly permitted by the 1976 Copyright Act or in writing from the publisher. Requests for permission should be addressed in writing to Permissions, Abingdon Press, 2222 Rosa L. Parks Blvd., PO Box 280988, Nashville, TN 37228-0988, or e-mailed to permissions@abingdonpress.com.

This book is printed on acid-free paper.

Library of Congress Cataloging-in-Publication Data has been requested.

ISBN: 978-1-4267-6639-8

Unless otherwise indicated, all scripture is from the New Revised Standard Version of the Bible, copyright 1989, Division of Christian Education of the National Council of the Churches of Christ in the United States of America. Used by permission. All rights reserved.

Scripture quotations marked KJV are from The Authorized (King James) Version. Rights in the Autho-rized Version in the United Kingdom are vested in the Crown. Reproduced by permission of the Crown's patentee, Cambridge University Press.

Scripture quotations marked NASB are taken from the New American Standard Bible® (NASB), Copy-right © 1960, 1962, 1963, 1968, 1971, 1972, 1973, 1975, 1977, 1995 by The Lockman Foundation. Used by permission. www.Lockman.org

Scripture quotations noted CEB are taken from the Common English Bible, copyright 2011. Used by permission. All rights reserved.

Scripture quotations marked (NIV) are taken from the Holy Bible, New International Version®, NIV®. Copyright © 1973, 1978, 1984, 2011 by Biblica, Inc.™ Used by permission of Zondervan. All rights reserved worldwide. www.zondervan.com The "NIV" and "New International Version" are trademarks registered in the United States Patent and Trademark Office by Biblica, Inc.™

17 18 19 20 21 22 23 24 25 26—10 9 8 7 6 5 4 3 2 1
MANUFACTURED IN THE UNITED STATES OF AMERICA

for the others among "us"

Contents

Acknowledgments

Many thanks to Warren Carter for the invitation to write for the Abingdon Core Biblical Studies series and for David Teel's kind support through the writing process. Warren provided quick and judicious feedback on my work, which is certainly stronger because of his efforts. Thanks also to Laura Wheeler at Abingdon Press and Kevin Harvey for their good work in bringing the manuscript to production. As always, I am grateful to my department colleagues at Seton Hall University for their ongoing collegiality and support of my scholarship. And, no book of mine would be complete if I did not express my heartfelt thanks to David Carr. Not many scholars are fortunate enough to have a spouse who reads early versions of chapters *and* finds them interesting enough to talk about over breakfast or an evening glass of wine. For his constant love and support, always thoughtful reading, and helpful suggestions, I am grateful.

I have always struggled with the dualism of the Johannine Literature and perhaps no more so than during the writing of this book. At a time of intense division in the political landscape of the United States, I have been painfully aware of the way the Johannine literature divides the world into "us" and "them." It is for this reason that I dedicate my work to individuals who feel that they are relegated to the outside, whoever they may be, even as they live and work among "us."

General Preface

This book, part of the Core Biblical Studies series, is designed as a starting point for New Testament study.

The volumes that constitute this series function as gateways. They provide entry points into the topics, methods, and contexts that are central to New Testament studies. They open up these areas for inquiry and understanding.

In addition, they are guidebooks for the resulting journey. Each book seeks to introduce its readers to key concepts and information that assist readers in the process of making meaning of New Testament texts. The series takes very seriously the importance of these New Testament texts, recognizing that they have played and continue to play a vital role in the life of faith communities and indeed in the larger society. Accordingly, the series recognizes that important writings need to be understood and wrestled with, and that the task of meaning making is complicated. These volumes seek to be worthy guides for these efforts.

The volumes also map out pathways. Previous readers in various contexts and circumstances have created numerous pathways for engaging the New Testament texts. Pathways are methods or sets of questions or perspectives that highlight dimensions of the texts. Some methods focus on the worlds behind the texts, the contexts from which they emerge and especially the circumstances of the faith communities to which they were addressed. Other methods focus on the text itself and the world that the text constructs. And some methods are especially oriented to the locations and interests of readers, the circumstances and commitments that readers bring to the text in interacting with it. The books in this series cannot engage every dimension of the complex meaning-making task, but they can lead readers along some of these pathways. And they can point to newer pathways that encourage further explorations relevant to this cultural moment. This difficult and complex task of interpretation is always an unfolding path as readers in different contexts and with diverse concerns and questions interact with the New Testament texts.

A series that can be a gateway, provide a guide, and map out pathways provides important resources for readers of the New Testament. This is what these volumes seek to accomplish.

Warren Carter
General Editor, New Testament
Core Biblical Studies

Chapter 1
Getting to Know the Johannine Literature

Readers cannot understand any part of the Gospel of John until they understand the whole.[1]

This book has two main goals: (1) to introduce you to the Gospel and Letters of John and (2) to introduce you to the different ways biblical scholars study these texts. The first step in this process is for you to get better acquainted with these ancient texts. And by this I mean, reading them from beginning to end before we begin to explore them more deeply. This way, you can have a sense of the whole of these writings before we look at their individual parts.

To help you with this first step, this chapter provides a basic reading guide for the Gospel and the Letters of John. As you move through the guide, you will see suggested reading assignments along with questions to consider as you read. If you are used to studying the Bible primarily in devotional settings, these questions will begin to introduce you to the academic study of the Johannine writings. If you are completely unfamiliar with these writings, the reading guide will help you notice details that you might not have noticed otherwise.

Don't worry if you don't know the answers to the questions. For now, the main point is simply to become familiar with the Gospel and the Letters and to stir your curiosity about what you find. And if you find yourself asking additional questions about what you are reading, then you're on the right track! One last point. In this initial reading process, I will occasionally point to certain types of questions that relate to the different scholarly approaches we will introduce in the rest of the book. Think of these glimpses at historical, literary, theological, and ideological questions as a preview of the coming attractions in the rest of the book.

Before beginning, I need to make a few points about terminology that I use in the book. The first point concerns the other three canonical Gospels, Mark, Matthew, and Luke. Scholars refer to these latter three Gospels as the "Synoptic Gospels." "Syn-optic" means something like "see together" in Greek. The Gospels of Mark, Matthew, and Luke "see" the story of Jesus in similar ways. We now know that this is because the authors of Matthew and Luke used the Gospel of Mark as one of their sources. The Gospel of John is not part of this "seeing together" group. It is very different than the other three Gospels in many ways. In this sense, it is a "maverick gospel" as one scholar tagged it. Part of my task in the book is to help you see the Gospel of John in all of its often mysterious differentness. Thus, we will have regular occasions to compare the Gospel of John with the Synoptic Gospels.

The second point concerns references to the Gospel of John and to Jesus as he is depicted in the Gospel. There is a long tradition of referring to this last canonical Gospel as the "Fourth Gospel." I will do so occasionally, just for the sake of variety in your reading experience. At times, I will refer to Jesus as "the Johannine Jesus" and sometimes simply as Jesus. The first is meant as a reminder that the Jesus under discussion is the one who is depicted in the Fourth Gospel. This Jesus says and does things differently than the "Markan Jesus," the "Matthean Jesus," or the "Lukan Jesus," that is, the various literary renditions of Jesus in the Synoptic Gospels. Because I must refer to Jesus many times in the book, I won't always use the more cumbersome "Johannine Jesus," but you should keep in mind that this is the figure under discussion.

On Terminology: "Criticism"

Academic approaches to the Bible are referred to as different types of biblical "criticism." One who uses these approaches is a "critic." These terms have nothing to do with attacking or "criticizing" the Bible, as the common uses of these terms might suggest. Rather, a biblical critic is one who engages in an analytic investigation of the text and thinks "critically" about various interpretive problems and solutions.

Getting to Know the Gospel of John

There are many ways one could outline the Gospel of John. For our purposes, we will use the following broad divisions for this initial reading of the Gospel as a whole.

I. The *Logos* Enters the World (1:1-18)

II. Signs and Revelation in the World (1:19–5:47)

III. Growing Division and Opposition to Jesus (6–12)

IV. Preparation for Departure from the World (13–17)

V. The Hour of Departure (18–21)

The Logos *Enters the World (1:1-18)*

Read John 1:1-18

What claims are made about the "Word"? What is the relationship between the Word and God? What is the relationship between the Word and Jesus? What story do these verses tell?

The Gospel of John begins "in the beginning," an opening phrase that recalls Genesis 1:1. These first eighteen verses of the Gospel are commonly called the Prologue. This is because this opening section stands apart from the rest of the narrative while introducing its major themes. The Prologue goes on to describe the Word (Greek, *logos*)—how it relates to God and what it does. Although many English translations use the pronoun "he," as in the NRSV, "He was in the beginning with God," the

3

Greek pronoun used here relates back to the Word. The sentence is more accurately translated, "It was in the beginning with God." Or, we might read with the King James Version, "The same was in the beginning…" This way of translating the verse makes clear that this initial reference is to the preexistent *logos* rather than to the man Jesus. The implications of this poetic opening is that it takes the reader back to a time before time— indeed a time before creation. Note the other terms used to describe this *logos*—life and light. While the term *logos* does not reappear in the rest of the Gospel, we will see recurring references to both life and light. Here the *creative* function of this Word/Light is highlighted twice (1:2, 10). These opening lines present the reader with the Gospel's first paradox. Not only is the Word *with* God in the beginning, it *is* God. There is no further explanation for how both of these are true.

Notice that the Prologue progresses in a cyclical rather than linear way. At 1:9, the "true light" is coming into the world. Verses 10-13 concern knowledge, rejection versus acceptance of this light by others. Here we learn of the benefits of belief in "his name" (which has not yet been mentioned), receiving power to become children of God. Verse 14 then circles *back* to the idea of the Word coming into the world. The language shifts to a first-person account: "the Word became flesh and lived among us [Gk. *eskēnōsen*, literally, pitched a tent] and we have seen his glory." Note that later in the book, I will return to this verse because it is central to the debate among interpreters about how to understand the significance of Jesus in the Gospel.

One other example of the circular pattern in the Prologue is seen in the introduction of a "man named John" at verses 6-8 and then a second mention of him at verse 15. This man named John is the same figure as John the Baptist in the Synoptic Gospels, but he is never called "the Baptist" in this Gospel. Here he is a witness, who has come to testify to the light. Note that the writer takes pains to make clear that John is *not* the light. Verse 15 provides the actual words of testimony, which again emphasize Jesus's superiority over John. Verse 16 then returns to the "we" of verse 14, again describing the benefits received from Jesus, who is only finally named in the next verse.

The Prologue concludes by first distinguishing the role of Moses as lawgiver from that of Jesus, who brings grace and truth (1:16-17). It then distinguishes Jesus from every other human being. This "only begotten" one (either "Son" or "God"—the oldest copies of the Gospel differ on this point) is intimately close to God's "heart" (Gk: *kolpos* = breast or bosom).

Signs and Revelation in the World (1:19–5:47)

Read John 1:19–5:47

What does the character named John do and say in this section? What is his role in the story? Make a list of the "signs" that Jesus does. What effect do they have? When does Jesus travel to Jerusalem? What does he do there?

Following the Prologue, the story of Jesus's ministry begins. There is no story of Jesus's birth in the Gospel of John (cp. Matt 1–2; Luke 1–2). More like the Gospel of Mark, the story begins with John heralding the coming of Jesus. But before this happens, John has an exchange with a group of priests and Levites who had been sent from Jerusalem by "the Jews." This group (*hoi Iudaioi* in Greek) appears here for the first time in the Gospel and will eventually become the major opposition group to Jesus. The reference to "priests and Levites" suggests a connection with the Jerusalem temple authorities. Note that John refers to their question "Who are you?" in an odd way. Rather than offer a positive identification, he responds with a doubly negative acknowledgment or confession. "He confessed and did not deny, but confessed, 'I am not the Messiah'" (1:20).

---

hoi Iudaioi and "The Jews"

The phrase *hoi Iudaioi* is a highly problematic term in the Gospel of John, one that has generated much scholarly attention and debate. It is a notoriously difficult phrase to translate for several reasons. Literally, the phrase means "the Judeans," as in "the inhabitants of Judea." But, the term had more than just a geographical meaning, since ancient Greek writers also used it to refer to adherents of Judaism. In the ancient world, this would not simply describe a religious affiliation, but also a social, ethnic, and political affiliation. Significantly, it is a term that would apply to the historical Jesus and his disciples (even though they were not from Judea). Most English translations of the Greek text render *hoi Iudaioi* with the phrase "the Jews" (but without quotation marks). In the Gospel of John, the term is mostly used to refer to Jesus's opponents, but sometimes it seems to be a more neutral cultural identifier (for example, 2:6, 13), which just adds a degree of complication to the whole issue. Why the author designates this opposition group as *hoi Iudaioi* is a matter of scholarly debate, but simply using the phrase "the Jews" in connection with this group in the Gospel has had devastating consequences related to the history of Christian anti-Semitism. We will have occasion to reflect on the problem at various points in this introduction to the Fourth Gospel. My use of quotation marks around the translation "the Jews" throughout this book is to remind readers of the problems connected to the phrase.

This is the third time that the Gospel writer has called attention to what John is *not*. Why do you think this is? Scholars who are interested in the historical events lying behind the Gospel notice details like these because they suggest there is some underlying historical issue about the relationship between John and Jesus. Much later in the book, in chapter 5, we will return to this point.

Thinking like a Critic

At this point, take a moment to think as a historical critic does. Form a hypothesis about what might have been true historically about the figure of John in relation to Jesus.

The first appearances of Jesus in the Gospel simply show him as walking and being noticed by others (1:35-37). Jesus's first words are "What are you looking for?" directed at the two men who are following him (1:38). This is how Jesus begins gathering disciples, starting with two of John's own disciples (1:35-39). There is no calling of the disciples, as we read about in the Synoptic Gospels (Mark 1:16-20; Matt 4:18-22). In John, the soon-to-be disciples are attracted to him, call him by special titles, and begin to witness to other men about what they have seen. In this way, they continue the pattern set by John of witnessing about Jesus.

Chapter 2 narrates events that occur on "the third day" when Jesus performs what is called his "first sign" at a wedding at Cana, a small town in Galilee. The story is remarkable for several reasons. The first is the odd exchange between Jesus and his mother. She lets him know that the wine has run out, as if he is the host at the wedding. He, calling her "woman," basically retorts that the wine problem is no concern of theirs. Jesus's mother appears to ignore this dismissal. She proceeds as though he will fix the problem, which, in fact, he does. Not only that, he provides an enormous amount of wine for the wedding, somewhere between 120 to 130 gallons! And very good wine, at that. This extraordinary amount of wine suggests there may be something more to the story than its literal meaning. In any case, the narrator reports that when Jesus performed this "sign," it revealed his glory and caused his disciples to believe in him. These three ideas—signs, glory, belief—will be important themes in the rest of the Gospel.

Following this first sign, Jesus travels to Jerusalem, going up during the Passover festival. He then causes a disturbance in the Jerusalem temple, driving out money changers and overturning tables (2:14-22). Here is a first glimpse of the tension between Jesus and the Jewish authorities. They are on the scene asking Jesus to explain his behavior. He does so in a riddling sort of way that they do not understand (2:18-20). This way of communicating is the beginning of a pattern that runs through the Gospel. As we will see, studying how and why the Gospel writer presents Jesus as speaking in enigmatic ways is of interest to both historical and literary critics of the Gospel. As I will discuss more in chapter 3, literary critics are interested in how the narrative of the Gospel combines different elements to convey its meaning.

Chapters 3 and 4 feature conversations between Jesus and two characters who appear only in the Gospel of John—Nicodemus and an unnamed woman from Samaria. Both conversations proceed by means of questions and responses from Jesus that seem to confuse these dialogue partners more than enlighten them. In both cases, Jesus appears to be speaking on a figurative level, teaching about attaining eternal life, while Nicodemus and the Samaritan woman understand him more literally. Nicodemus wonders how one can physically be born a second time, while the Samaritan woman asks for a flowing water supply that will reduce her workload. Again, exploring how the literal and figurative language function in this section requires a literary-critical approach to the Gospel.

Note that in John 4:27, when the disciples return to Jesus, they wonder why he is talking to a woman. This highlights for the reader what the woman has already made clear earlier in the conversation with Jesus—that it is unusual for him to be speaking with her (4:9). Ideological critics, those who are interested in exploring how cultural ideas and biases are reproduced in cultural texts, take notice of verses like these in the Gospel. In particular, this calls for exploration of what ideas about gender the Gospel is communicating and why. What does it mean that Jesus's disciples question his actions (but not directly)? What *is* the significance of the Johannine Jesus talking to a woman in this scene? We will return to these questions in chapter 5 of this book.

Returning to our read through the Gospel, notice that the first water-into-wine sign is followed by a second sign in 4:46-54. In this case, Jesus heals the son of a royal official from a distance. The restoration of his son brings the man and his household to belief. Here, though, a puzzling element is added to the story. When the man asks for healing for his son, Jesus appears to reprimand not only the royal official, but anyone who asks for "signs and wonders" (the "you" of 4:48 is plural in the Greek text).

Although these signs are designated as the first and the second signs, they are not the only signs mentioned in the section. In 2:23, many in Jerusalem believe in Jesus because of the signs he was doing. Looking ahead to the next section, Jesus draws a crowd because of the signs he is doing for the sick (6:2).

Finally, note one other element in this section. While Jesus is busy performing signs and bringing people to belief in him, he also ignites opposition. As I mentioned previously, there are hints of this already in chapter 2 when the temple authorities question Jesus about his actions. This tension builds through this section. In chapter 5, Jesus heals on the Sabbath. His opponents see him as working on the Sabbath and thereby violating Sabbath law, which renders it a day of rest. Even more, because Jesus calls God "Father," they see him as making himself "equal to God." For this reason, his opponents plan "all the more to kill him" (5:18). At this point in the Gospel, Jesus begins an extensive explanation regarding his relationship to God, or as he puts it, of the Son to the Father (5:19-47). This is not the only time Jesus will speak in detail, defending himself from his accusations against opponents. Here, and in other places, the language of the Gospel sounds decidedly juridical, with references to witnesses, testimony, accusers, and judgment.

Growing Division and Opposition to Jesus (6–12)

===

Read John 6–12 and Consider the Following Questions:

Which of the stories in these chapters are familiar to you from the other Gospels? Do you notice anything different about how these stories are told in the Gospel of John? What themes do you see developing in these chapters? Who are Jesus's opponents in these chapters? What reasons are given for the conflict between Jesus and the opponents he faces?

===

Chapter 6 tells a story about Jesus feeding a crowd of five thousand people, a tradition you may well be familiar with from the other canonical Gospels. In the Synoptic Gospels, Jesus has compassion on the crowd and urges his disciples to feed them so that the crowd does not have to go away looking for food (Mark 6:34-44; Matt 14:14-21; Luke 9:10-17). In the Gospel of John, Jesus "tests" the disciples before performing what is later identified as another sign (6:5-6). Moreover, in the Gospel of John, the feeding of the crowd shows the people that Jesus is "the prophet who is to come into the world" and they want to make him king (6:14-15). Moreover, this is not the end of the story in John. Jesus eventually challenges the motives of the crowd and offers another extended discourse about the "bread of heaven" (6:26-66).

This "bread of heaven" discourse builds on themes already introduced in the Gospel. Once again, Jesus refers to the possibility of eternal life for those who believe (6:40, 47-48). And again he finds himself contending with "the Jews" who, in this case, "murmur" against him (6:41). Note that this is the same word used in Exodus 17:3 when the Israelites complain against Moses. So we see yet another way that the Gospel draws a comparison between Jesus and Moses, who by the first century CE was a highly esteemed figure in the Jewish tradition. This time, Jesus's superiority to Moses is drawn even more sharply than in the Prologue (6:31-32, 48-49; cp. 1:16-17).

In chapter 7, Jesus's brothers urge him to attend another upcoming festival in Jerusalem and to make his works public. Much like his response to his mother in chapter 2, Jesus refuses because mysteriously his time has not yet come. And also as in chapter 2, Jesus goes on to do what they asked anyway. What makes Jesus's actions in chapter 7 especially enigmatic is that although he goes up "in secret" to Jerusalem, he soon teaches openly in the temple. In another indication of the rising conflict, Jesus's presence there sets off another round of division and uncertainty among the crowd (7:12-13, 40-43) with some of the temple police wanting to arrest him (7:44-48). The points of debate are the origin and identity of Jesus, in spite of Jesus's repeated claims about who he is and where he comes from. The negative reactions to Jesus show how the rejection of him that was anticipated in the Prologue is being played out in the narrative.

An Independent Jesus Tradition

Chapter 8 opens with a well-known story of Jesus's refusal to condemn a woman who has been caught in an adulterous act. As fascinating as this story is, we will not discuss it here. If you are using a study Bible such as the NRSV or the NIV you might have noticed brackets around 8:3-11. This is to indicate that this story does not appear in the earliest copies of the Gospel. Not only that, in some manuscripts it appears in a different place in the Gospel of John. The story also shows up in some manuscript copies of the Gospel of Luke. This suggests that the story circulated independently before scribes began to insert it into different places in the Gospels of Luke and John. At some point, the story settled into its current location in John 8.

Studying ancient manuscripts to discover the original content of a biblical text is called textual criticism. We will see more examples of this type of work later in this book.

Beginning with John 8:12, the narrative returns to a dispute with "the Jews," and the courtroom-type language that we saw in chapter 5. There Jesus suggests that it is not legitimate to testify on his own behalf (5:31). Here, "the Jews" raise the same objection but at this point Jesus insists that he can testify because "I know where I have come from and where I am going, but you do not know where I come from or where I am going" (8:14). Notably, he also refers to "your law" when he is speaking with the Jews, a peculiar reference since Jesus himself is Jewish. The vitriolic rhetoric builds throughout this chapter, with Jesus eventually suggesting that the Jews are not the children of Abraham nor of God. He says they are children of the devil, "a murderer" and "the father of lies" (8:31-44).

For contemporary readers, this heated rhetoric is disturbing, given the long, dark history of anti-Semitism in the Christian tradition. As I will discuss later in the book, especially in light of the genocide of millions of Jewish people by Nazi Germany, scholars feel morally obligated to understand why this language is present in the Gospel.

The transition from chapter 8 to 9 is rather abrupt, but the story in chapter 9 about the man born blind continues the theme of the strong opposition between Jesus and "the Jews." This healing story is an excellent example of the distinctive way the Gospel presents the miraculous acts (signs) of Jesus. In each case, it is not simply the act that is significant.

Even more important is the interpretation of the event by Jesus and/or the narrator as well as the reaction to the event by those who witness it. In chapter 9, the healing of the blind man takes up just two verses (9:6-7), while the entire rest of the chapter is devoted to conflict and conversation about the meaning of the healing and what it suggests about the healer. In fact, the discussion that Jesus has with his disciples before the healing already begins to interpret the act—the man was born blind so that God's works would be revealed in his eventual healing by Jesus (9:1-5). The healing itself then leads to a dispute (again!) about the identity and origin of Jesus. Is he a sinner who willfully dishonors the Sabbath or is he a man sent from God?

The chapter unfolds in a series of conversations, between the man, his neighbors, the Pharisees (or "Jews" as they are also called), and the man's parents. Notably, the parents are afraid to answer questions about their son, because, as the narrator reports, "the Jews had already agreed that anyone who confessed Jesus to be the Messiah would be put out of the synagogue" (9:22). This decision is nowhere related in earlier parts of the Gospel, nor is it mentioned anywhere else in the New Testament writings. As we will see, this particular verse has been the source of much debate in scholarship on the Gospel. Here we will just note that Jesus, who has been absent across these interrogations, reappears again only after the man has defended Jesus and consequently been "put out" by the Jews. The story concludes with the man's confession of faith in Jesus and Jesus's pronouncement about his opponents' "blindness."

John 10 contains a well-known image of Jesus—Jesus as a good shepherd (10:11, 14). Less known is that he also says he is the gate for the sheep (10:7, 9), asserting that it is through him that his followers can be saved. Using the image of the shepherd, Jesus also insists that no one takes his life from him. He lays his life down for his sheep. Thus, just as Jesus interprets his signs before they happen, in this discourse, he anticipates his crucifixion and preemptively interprets it as a voluntary death for the sake of his sheep (see also 15:13).

This section of the Gospel concludes with chapters 11 and 12. The events of this chapter signal that the narrative is at a point of transition.

Chapter 11 relates what some scholars count as the seventh and last of the signs that are narrated in the Gospel—the raising of Lazarus from the dead. As with all of the signs of Jesus, this particular one is meant to point to a truth about Jesus. He explains to his disciples that the point of Lazarus's illness (and death) is the glorification of God, and thereby also of God's Son (11:4, 40).

Indeed, this particularly dramatic sign foreshadows Jesus's own death and resurrection. Notice that, like Jesus, Lazarus is buried in the tomb for several days before Jesus calls him from the tomb. The story refers to the burial wrappings of Lazarus using the same term that appears in 20:7 to refer to Jesus's burial wrappings. The most explicit link between the healing and Jesus is made by Jesus himself. As in chapter 9, Jesus offers an interpretation of what will take place through a prior dialogue—in this case, it is with Martha, the sister of Lazarus. Jesus explains, "I am the resurrection and the life. Those who believe in me, even though they die, will live" (11:25). In response to this, Martha offers the fullest confession of faith that we find in the narrative (11:27).

Jesus's death is also foreshadowed in John 12:1-8, where Jesus interprets Mary's anointing of his feet with oil as an anticipation of his burial (12:7). This anointing story is another tradition that is common to all four Gospels. In the Johannine version, the anointing story and Jesus's procession into Jerusalem are both linked to this Gospel's unique story of the raising of Lazarus. The anointing takes place at Lazarus's house (12:1). Afterward, the crowds who come out to see Jesus enter Jerusalem are there because they heard that Lazarus was raised from the dead (12:7-18). The significance of the story is further reinforced when the authorities plot not only to put Jesus to death but also to kill Lazarus! And there is another interesting detail in this lead-up to Jesus's arrest, trial, and crucifixion. Only in the Fourth Gospel do the Jewish leaders point to their fear of Rome as a reason for putting Jesus to death (11:48). This detail has historical significance and we return to it several times later in the book.

Finally, the closing verses of the chapter reinforce the sense that a shift is occurring at this part of the story. Jesus, who supposedly has departed and is in hiding (12:36), now "cries out with a loud voice," almost as if from offstage (12:44-50). He repeats much of what he has already taught, offering a summary of his message, before the Gospel takes a turn in the next chapter.

Preparation for Departure from the World (13–17)

Read Chapters 13–17

What happens during Jesus's meal with his disciples? What is the "new commandment" that Jesus gives to his disciples? How does Jesus describe the relationship between God, Jesus, and his followers? What does Jesus tell his followers they can expect after his departure? What will the "advocate" do for followers of Jesus? (The NRSV translates the Greek word *parakletos* as Advocate. Other translations use "Comforter" or "Helper" or "Companion.")

If chapters 11 and 12 anticipate a shift in the story, chapter 13 decisively marks the occurrence of that shift. After several earlier claims by the Johannine Jesus that his time had not yet come (2:4; 7:30; 8:20), he now knows that his time to depart and return to the Father has arrived (13:1). In the chapters that follow (13–17), Jesus prepares his closest disciples for what is to come. Once again, the Gospel has hints of overlap with the other Gospels, but differs from them in significant ways. Across the four Gospels, Jesus has a parting meal with his disciples (Mark 14:22-25; Matt 26:26-29; Luke 22:15-20). John's version differs in a number of ways, which we discuss more in the next chapter. Among the most significant is that, in the Gospel, the meal does not become a memorial meal for Jesus over bread and wine. Instead, the Johannine Jesus washes his disciples' feet, telling them, "So if I, your Lord and Teacher, have washed your feet, you also ought to wash one another's feet" (13:14). This emphasis on service to one another points ahead to the "new commandment" that Jesus will soon give to his disciples to "love one another" (13:34-35).

Jesus's preparation for his departure continues in chapters 14–17. These chapters, commonly known as the "farewell discourse," convey

14

overarching themes of love and comfort promised to Jesus's believers, in stark contrast to the alienation and hate they will experience in the world. More than once, the Johannine Jesus highlights the parallel relationships between the Father, Jesus, and his disciples, assuring them that if they keep his commandments, they will be loved by Jesus and the Father (15:9-10). Jesus's promises that he will not leave them "orphans" indicates the familiar relationship this Gospel has in view between Father, Son, and followers of Jesus. More specifically, it recalls the claim from the Prologue that believers would become children of God (1:12). The Johannine Jesus promises to send his disciples an "Advocate" who will help them in their struggle in the world. This is a distinctive figure in the Fourth Gospel who relates to the time after the death of Jesus. I will return to discussing the Advocate in our exploration of the Gospel's ideas of the church community.

The Hour of Departure (18–21)

Read John 18–21

Pay special attention to events at Jesus' arrest. What stands out in this scene? What do you think the storyteller is trying to convey in this scene?

The final chapters of the Gospel tell the story of Jesus's passion. The broad strokes of this story are the same across the four canonical Gospels. Jesus is arrested, questioned by Jewish and Roman authorities, handed over to die by the Roman governor, Pontius Pilate, and crucified by the Roman authorities. But the Gospel of John differs from the Synoptic Gospels in its presentation of Jesus. The Johannine Jesus often gives the impression that he is in control of the events taking place.

For instance, the story of Jesus's arrest is told in a way that makes Jesus assist in his own capture. He comes forward to meet the large contingent of men who come to arrest him. When he identifies himself, they fall to the ground with his words "I am," indicating his unique and authoritative status. Only the Fourth Gospel features an extended trial before Pilate. The trial unfolds in a series of scenes with the Roman governor shuttling between inside his headquarters to speak with Jesus and outside to address "the Jews" (18:28–19:16). Throughout it all, Jesus appears unfazed. He tells Pilate that whatever power Pilate is currently wielding over him is only because he has been given it "from above" (19:11). This Gospel alone recounts the scene where Jesus arranges for his mother to be taken into the home of his disciple (19:26-27). Finally, the Johannine Jesus dies by giving up his spirit only when he knows that all has been finished (19:30).

In the Gospel of John, the empty tomb scene also differs from the synoptic traditions. Whereas the other canonical Gospels all feature several women present together at the tomb of Jesus after his death, in the Fourth Gospel, only Mary Magdalene goes alone to the tomb. It is true that Peter and the beloved disciple race to the tomb when Mary reports to them that she has found it empty. And this race is crafted in a way to award some special privilege to each male disciple—Peter arrives first, but the beloved disciple enters the tomb first. Neither one, however, sees the risen Jesus. The narrative reserves that privilege for Mary Magdalene, who remains at the tomb alone. Indeed, Jesus appears first to Mary Magdalene, who recognizes Jesus once he calls her by name (10:3). Mary's role is to convey news of Jesus's resurrection to his "brothers." While she does make this announcement, the narrative includes no response from the disciples. Instead the scene shifts to two more resurrection appearances. Jesus appears first to the disciples behind locked doors, then a week later to Thomas.

Here the Gospel appears to move toward a conclusion. At 20:31, the writer tells his audience that Jesus did many other signs in the presence of his disciples and suggests that the ones that were described in the Gospel have been told so the audience either will come to belief or continue to believe in Jesus (the Greek manuscript traditions vary on the verb tense).

In either case, what sounds like a conclusion turns out not to be a conclusion. Another chapter (21) appears to sort out potential questions about Peter (what happened to him after this threefold denial of his discipleship?) and rumors about the disciple whom Jesus loved (didn't Jesus say he wasn't going to die?). Once these issues have been treated, the Gospel concludes for good. This final verse uses the first-person "I suppose" to comment about Jesus's abundant deeds—no books could be written that could contain all of them!

Getting to Know the Johannine Letters

Although 1 John traditionally has been called a letter, it lacks the formal structure and elements of an ancient letter. There is no sender or recipient mentioned, no words of greeting, no mention of wishes to be with the audience in person, or direct requests, no greetings sent from third parties (all elements found, for example, in Paul's letters, such as 1 Thessalonians). In this sense, 1 John is not so much a letter, as an exhortation or instructional writing to an unidentified audience. In fact, some have suggested that 1 John is more sermon than letter, but this does not take account of the self-consciously *written* nature of the document. The author repeats the fact that he is writing thirteen times (1:4; 2:1, 7-8, 12-14, 21, 26; 5:13)! Moreover, the writer addresses his audience in a way that seems to be responding to particular events about which they are familiar, much like a letter might do. Given this, and the fact that tradition has named 1 John an "epistle," we will refer to it this way for the purposes of our discussion.

Read 1 John

This writing is often referred to as a letter. Does it have a letter form? Who is writing to whom? Is there a particular situation that is being addressed? How would you describe the overall tone of the letter?

As with the Gospel, the name of the author is never mentioned. The opening line of 1 John simply refers to a "we," suggesting a group behind the writing who together address a "you" (Gk. plural). Later in the text, the author refers to himself as "I" (masc. singular) while referring regularly to his audience as "little children" or simply "children" (e.g., 1 John 2:1, 4, 12, 18; 3:7, 18).

Though the text is anonymous, it is easy to understand why readers have long associated 1 John with the Gospel of John. Both open with Prologues with references to the beginning, the word, life, as well as the Father and the Son (cp. John 1:1-5, 18 and 1 John 1:1). Such overlapping vocabulary is evident throughout these writings with references to light (1 John 1:5-6; 5:13), darkness (1 John 1:5-6; 2:8-9, 11), and truth (1 John 1:6, 8; 2:21; 3:19; 4:6). In the Gospel, Jesus also refers to his disciples as children, and indeed, the promise is that those who believe will become children of God. In terms of shared phrasing, examples include "walking in darkness," "conquering the world," "receiving witness," and "everyone who does sin." The author of 1 John writes so that his audience's "joy may be complete," much like the Johannine Jesus instructs his disciples to pray so that their joy can be complete (16:24). The Gospel and 1 John also share terms that occur nowhere else in the New Testament. Both refer to the Advocate (*parakleton*—John 14:16, 26; 15:26; 16:7 / 1 John 2:1). Both refer to "murderers" (John 8:44 / 1 John 3:15).

In the same way that there are strong overlaps with the Prologue, so also with the closing verse of each writing. These are not all the parallels between the writings, but the point is clear: the two are related in some way. And what is true of 1 John is also true of the two other letters. Even though 2 and 3 John are the shortest writings in the New Testament, they also draw on the same "Johannine" vocabulary. As George Parsenios observes, "Both texts refer to 'these things' that are 'written,' and both texts connect 'belief' in the 'Son of God' to 'having' either 'life' or 'eternal life.'"[2]

We will return to the question of the relationship between the Gospel and 1 John in chapter 6. For now, our aim is simply to become more familiar with 1 John, highlighting its major themes. Although it is difficult to discern a clear ordering to the writing, one can readily see certain ideas being repeated. Often the structure of the letter is described as a spiral, with the author repeatedly circling back to themes of abiding together in God's love. The outline below is designed to demonstrate the repeated reminders of the love shared in the community.

Prologue: the witness of the "word of life": 1:1-4

Recalling Jesus as a cleansing sacrifice for sins: 1:5–2:2

Obeying the commandment to love: 2:5-17

Warnings about the antichrist and deception: 2:18-23

Abiding in the love of God: 2:24–3:3

Defining those who sin versus those who cannot sin: 3:4-10

The message to love one another: 3:11-24

Warnings to test every spirit: 4:1-6

Admonitions to love one another: 4:7–5:13

Epilogue: sin and knowledge of the true God: 5:14-21

The main point of the prologue is to affirm the truth of preaching that they have heard. It does so by evoking sensory language of seeing and touching. This is not to indicate that they were actually present to see and touch Jesus, but to claim that the preaching they have heard about him evoked his presence in a very real way. Paul uses a similar kind of sensory language when he writes to the Galatians in 3:1 that "it was before your eyes that [he] was publically exhibited as crucified!" He does not mean that the Galatians were physically present at the crucifixion, but that his preaching about the death of Jesus brought the event "before their eyes." Following this opening, the author soon turns to concerns of "walking in darkness" and the idea of sin, reminding his readers about the cleansing sacrifice of Jesus (1 John 1:6-7). The theme of who can and cannot commit sin will preoccupy the author as the text continues, so this initial statement on the availability of forgiveness to his audience is significant.

The author distinguishes his readers on the basis of love and obedience to God. The readers—whom the author refers to not only as "little children" but also as "brothers" (3:13) and "beloved" (2:7; 3:2, 21; 4:1, 7, 11)—are those who obey the commandments of God (3:22), and in particular the "new commandment" to love one another (3:14). They know the truth because the spirit that they received abides in them (3:24). They are strong and have conquered the "evil one" (2:14). "We love," the author asserts, "because he first loved us" (4:19). At the same time the author describes his audience in this reassuring way, he exhorts them to continue on this same path. "Let us love," he proclaims (3:18; 4:17), reminding his readers six different times of their need to "love one another." By doing so, the author assures his readers, they can rest in the knowledge that they are righteous before God and have eternal life (2:25; 5:11, 13).

All this is stated clearly enough, but there are some puzzling aspects of the text, especially regarding the theme of sin in relation to the readers. As we have seen, the author reminds his audience that confessing sins offers a means of forgiveness because of Jesus's sacrifice. He also claims that to deny one's capacity for sin is to lie. On the other hand, he speaks of those who abide as *not* sinning (3:6), asserts that to commit sin is to be a "child of the devil," and further, that those born of God *cannot* sin (3:8-9). This is an interpretive crux in 1 John, and perhaps an unresolvable tension. We discuss it further in our last chapter of this book.

More straightforward in 1 John is the author's view of the distinction between his readers who are "from God" (4:4, 6) compared to those who are not from God but are "from the world" (4:5). The letter shares the same dualistic worldview of the Gospel. In this case, the world is described as a place of desire for material pleasure (2:15-16). "The world" does not know God nor recognize God's followers (3:1). It is transient compared to the eternal life of those who love God. They should not be surprised, according to the author, to find that the world hates them (3:13).

In the midst of this negative description of the world and those who live in it, the author speaks of a particular group of people who have left the community. The author associates this group with the problematic "world." "They went out from us," he writes, "but they did not belong to us; for if they had belonged to us, they would have remained with us" (2:19; see also 4:5). This reference to a group who has left has proved the most tantalizing for later readers of the letter. Who left and why? And what sort of community did they leave? As we will see, historical critics have proposed a number of ways to reconstruct the events behind this verse.

20

Read 2 and 3 John

What connection do you see between these brief letters and 1 John? What is distinctive about each one?

Unlike 1 John, these two documents clearly take the form of letters. The chart below shows how the Letters correspond to elements that were standard in Hellenistic letters.

	2 John		3 John
Prescript	Address: vv. 1-2		Address: v. 1
	Greeting: v. 3		Greeting: vv. 2-4
Body	vv. 4-11		vv. 5-12
Closing	vv. 12-13		vv. 13-15

In 2 John, we find a reference to the author, "the elder," and an addressee, "the elect lady and her children" (2 John 1:1). Third John provides an actual name for the addressee, a certain "beloved Gaius" (3 John 1:1). Thus, both appear to be personal letters to an individual, each dealing with particular situations. Second John uses language quite similar to 1 John. The writer refers to the love commandment (vv. 5-6) and warns against deceptive antichrists (v. 7). In the case of 3 John, there is a reference to a conflict with someone named Diotrephes and positive regard for someone else named Demetrius (both Greek names). The brevity and instructive style of these personal letters is conventional, as well as the concluding wish by the letter writer that he will soon be present and able to talk face to face with the recipient (2 John 12; 3 John 13-14).

Having come to the end of this initial read through the Johannine literature, we are now ready to explore it more deeply from several interpretive perspectives. We begin in the next chapter with historical questions about the Gospel of John.

Chapter 2

Exploring Historical Puzzles in the Gospel of John

If you are beginning this chapter, you hopefully have already read through the Gospel of John and the Johannine epistles, using the reading guide in the previous chapter. There I highlighted some of the unique characteristics of this literature. I especially noted the ways that the Gospel of John differs from the Synoptic Gospels. This chapter builds on that initial reading, now focusing on historical questions.

But what type of historical questions? We should be clear from the beginning that the primary emphasis is *not* on questions about the historical Jesus—that is, questions about what Jesus did and said during his ministry early in the first century CE. Rather, our interest will be on the historical circumstances that contributed to the composition of the Gospel of John. This is often described as the world behind the text.

As in the last chapter, the aim is to start with your own observations and reflections on certain pieces of textual evidence. This time, however, you will be accompanied by other scholars who have long pondered the questions that I will ask you to consider. I begin with observations about the Gospel that historical critics have found especially intriguing, and often puzzling.

Questions of Chronology

Comparing Gospel Chronologies

Skim through the Gospel and count how many times the Johannine Jesus attends the Passover festival in Jerusalem. Compare this to the references to the Passover festival in the Gospel of Mark (hint: the first reference to a festival in Mark is in chapter 14).

Compare also the following events in the two Gospels: when Jesus disrupts the temple practice (John 2 / Mark 11) and when Jesus has a final meal with his disciples (John 13, cp. to Mark 14:12ff and parallels).

As you likely noticed from these initial observations, there are substantial differences in the chronology of the Gospel of John compared to the Synoptic Gospels. Very early in the Gospel, Jesus goes to Jerusalem for the Passover and causes a controversial upheaval in the temple (2:13-23). In the Synoptic Gospels, a similar scene comes just before the passion narrative, but here the "temple cleansing" tradition appears at the outset of Jesus's ministry. Clearly, the author is not following a chronology of Jesus's life from the synoptic tradition. This is ever more apparent when we see that after this first eventful trip to Jerusalem, the narrator reports two more trips of Jesus to Jerusalem for the annual Passover festival (6:4; 11:55). This means that the ministry of Jesus spans more than two years in the Gospel of John. In contrast, the Synoptic Gospels reference only one trip to Jerusalem for the Passover, the one that results in Jesus's arrest and crucifixion. As we noticed in our initial reading of the Gospel, Jesus's farewell meal with his disciples is not a Passover meal. This means, as the narrator twice mentions, that Jesus's death takes place on the Jewish day of *preparation* for the Passover (19:14, 42).

Taken together, we have a key event taking place at a different point in Jesus's ministry, something closer to a three-year ministry of Jesus versus one year, and a final meal and crucifixion that takes place on different days. At this point we must consider, what types of historical questions do these textual observations raise?

Signs versus Miracles

The Johannine Jesus performs signs (Greek, *semeia*), rather than miracles (*dynamis*, "works of power"). The first of these occurs in 2:1-11 where Jesus turns water into wine at a wedding feast in Cana of Galilee. The narrative identifies this act as the first of Jesus's signs, which reveals his glory. The result is that his disciples believe in him (2:11).

In chapter 4, Jesus performs what is referred to as a second sign, again in Cana, where he heals a royal official's son. As with the first sign in Cana, the result of this one is that the official and his household believe in Jesus (4:46-54). Still, designation of this healing as a second sign is puzzling because there are two earlier references to the numerous signs that Jesus has been performing (2:23; 3:2).

After the narrating of Jesus's first and second sign, the enumerating of signs ends—we do not read of a "third" and "fourth" sign, and so forth. We do, however, read a good deal more about Jesus doing signs and what these signs suggest about who he is and where he comes from (see 6:2, 26; 7:31; 9:16; 11:47; 12:37, 47-48; 20:30-31). There is no disputing *that* the Johannine Jesus performs signs, but their implications and interpretation is a focus of much debate both internally to the Gospels, and in the world of Johannine scholarship.

In spite of several references to Jesus's "many signs," there are actually fewer narrated signs in the Gospel of John compared to Jesus's miracles in the Synoptic Gospels. Scholars typically count seven: the wedding at Cana, the raising of the royal official's son, healing the paralytic (5:1-15), feeding of five thousand (6:5-14), walking on water (6:16-24), healing the man born blind (9:1-7), and raising of Lazarus from the tomb (11:1-44). Some argue that the crucifixion/glorification of the Johannine Jesus should be considered the final sign. Others argue the "seven" is symbolically significant as the seven days of creation. In any case, there are significantly fewer healing stories than in the synoptic traditions, and there are no stories of exorcisms at all in the Fourth Gospel.

Nevertheless, while the author does not use the word *miracle* to describe Jesus's deeds, these fewer signs are in some ways "more miraculous" than Jesus's acts in the other Gospels. For example, whereas Jesus heals blind men in the synoptic traditions (Mark 8:22-25; Matt 10:46-52; 20:30-34; Luke 18:35-43), in the Gospel of John, the man who is healed has been blind since birth (9:1-7). Whereas Jesus brings a young girl from death to life in Mark 5:38-43, Markan Jesus's comment that she is not dead but sleeping, his arrangement of a private audience, and his order to say nothing about the miracle, contrasts sharply with the very public display of the Johannine Jesus calling Lazarus from a tomb after he has been dead and buried for four days (John 11:41-45).

There is also arguably a tension in the Gospel around the idea and purpose of the signs. In 4:48, Jesus appears to critique the father who needs signs to come to belief. Similarly, at the end of the Gospel, Jesus blesses those who come to belief without seeing (20:29). Although the word *semeia* ("sign") does not appear in this verse, it does appear in the very next verse. But, this concluding statement about signs recalls the positive purpose and assessment of signs with which the Gospel begins (2:11). According to the author, these "many signs" that are written in the Gospel are included to help people believe (20:30-31). There is some uncertainty about whether this verb means bringing people to belief, or helping believers maintain their faith, but in either case, the signs are meant to function in a positive way.[1]

A close look at the surrounding context for Jesus's signs reveals another way in which John's Gospel is distinct from the Synoptic Gospels. As I noted in the last chapter in relation to the healing of the man born blind, the narrating of the sign itself is often quite brief compared to the extensive discussion and controversy about the meaning and implications of the sign. We can see this pattern in several other places in the Gospel. John 6:1-2 relates a traditional story about Jesus feeding a multitude. This is a story that occurs in some form in all four of the Gospels, but in the Gospel of John, the feeding of the five thousand leads to an extensive dialogue between Jesus and the crowd. In the narrative, more than the actual sign, the discussion about Jesus as the bread of heaven is central (6:41-71).

One more example is the case of the raising of Lazarus. In this case, the statements that Jesus makes *before* the sign provide clues to the audience about its meaning even if the characters are unable to understand his statements (11:1-15, 20-27, 38-42).

Discourses versus Parables

In the Synoptic Gospels Jesus regularly teaches in parables. These short, trenchant narratives are typically used to convey a lesson about the nature of the kingdom of God and how one gains access to it. In the Gospel of John, however, the word *parable* never appears, nor does Jesus regularly use this genre to teach. The closest we come to this type of teaching occurs when the Johannine Jesus compares the combination of pain and joy his disciples will feel at his impending death and resurrection and the pain and joy of a woman giving birth (16:25). He refers to this as speaking in "figures" (16:25, Gk. *paromia*), but then says the hour is coming when he will speak "plainly." Soon enough in 16:29, the disciples confirm that now Jesus is speaking "plainly." A similar shift from figurative to plain speech occurs when the disciples misunderstand Jesus's description of Lazarus as "sleeping" (11:11-14). There Jesus tells them "plainly" that Lazarus is dead. In John 10:24, the Jews urge Jesus to tell them plainly whether he is the messiah, to which Jesus responds that he *has* told them and they didn't believe (10:25).

This last example points to the nature of Jesus's speech in the Gospel of John. He speaks often about his identity in extended discourses filled with symbolic and metaphorical descriptions. Frequently, these come in the form of "I am" statements. Jesus says, for example, that he is the bread of life, the light of the world, the door, the good shepherd, as well as other more abstract ideas such as "the resurrection, and the truth." We explore further this symbolic language in chapter 4. Here we simply note it as a distinctive way that the Johannine Jesus communicates compared to the Jesus of the synoptic tradition.

Problems with Coherence

Another set of observations does not involve comparison with the Synoptic Gospels, but simply a close reading of the narrative of the Gospel.

27

In several places, something unexpected occurs that disrupts the flow of the story. The most obvious instance of this comes at the end of chapter 14. Here Jesus has been comforting his disciples about his impending departure. At 14:30-31, he seems to bring his teaching to a close, telling them that he will no longer talk much with them and then instructs them, "Rise, let us be on our way." What would you expect to happen in the story after this command? Most readers would anticipate movement by the characters. But what comes next does not seem to be any sort of rising and departing. Instead, Jesus goes on talking, beginning a discourse about the true vine (15:1ff). This discourse continues through the next two chapters before moving into a prayer in chapter 17. Only at the beginning of chapter 18, "after he had spoken these words," do we read of the disciples going out with Jesus to a garden. Moreover, 16:4-33 essentially restates 14:1-31.

Also puzzling is Jesus's claim in 16:5, "None of you asks me where I am going," even though in 13:36, Peter asks exactly this and soon after, Thomas expresses concerns about the same thing (14:5). Such observations lead scholars to wonder about the composition of this section of the Gospel. What would cause a narrative to take the shape that this one does? Such questions become even more acute when we look toward the end of the Gospel. In 20:31 the narrator appears to bring the Gospel to a fitting conclusion with the following words: "Now Jesus did many other signs in the presence of his disciples, which are not written in this book. But these are written so that you may come to believe that Jesus is the Messiah, the Son of God, and that through believing you may have life in his name" (20:30-31).

Logically, most readers would expect the Gospel to come to a conclusion with these words. Instead, the narrative continues into another chapter where Jesus makes yet another appearance to his disciples and has another exchange with Peter. Only then does the Gospel finally conclude. Again, this double ending has led scholars to wonder about how the Gospel reached its final form.

If we read even more closely, there are other puzzling aspects of the narrative flow having to do with Jesus's travels. In 4:43, the narrator reports that Jesus travels from Samaria to Galilee. Then, in chapter 5, Jesus goes up to Jerusalem (which means going back through Samaria) where he heals a paralytic on the Sabbath, stirring controversy with the Jewish leaders. It is plausible to imagine Jesus traveling from Jerusalem to Samaria to Galilee and then back to Jerusalem again. But then, we suddenly read that Jesus goes to "the other side of the sea of Galilee." Granted, one needs a sense of Palestinian geography to appreciate what is odd about this. But if you imagine reading about Jesus's activity in New York City followed by a report that he then crossed to the other side of Lake Erie, you will understand the problem.

The Questions and Some Proposed Solutions

Clearly these observations about the Gospel open up a whole range of historically related questions. Students who are new to the study of the Gospels are often most concerned with questions of historical accuracy. Given these significant differences between the Johannine tradition and Synoptic Gospels, readers often want to know which tradition is the most historically credible.

From our twenty-first-century perspective, this is a reasonable question to ask and deserves careful consideration. It may be comforting to know that some ancient readers were also concerned about the differences they perceived between John and the Synoptic Gospels. At least one ancient writer seems aware that the differences could potentially raise questions about the authority of the Gospel of John. According to the early church historian Eusebius, a second-century bishop named Clement described the writing of the Gospel in his *Ecclesiastical History* as follows: "But, the last of all, John perceiving that the external facts had been made plain in the Gospels, being urged by his friends, and inspired by the Spirit, composed a spiritual Gospel" (6.14.7).

Most readers have understood Clement to mean that the Synoptic Gospels were reporting the historical facts about Jesus while John wrote to communicate his christological and theological significance. For many years, this assessment of the "spiritualizing" in the Gospel provided a satisfying reason for the distinctiveness of the Gospel of John. When historical criticism of the Gospels emerged in the eighteenth century, the spiritual

view of the Gospel carried over to the assumption that it was less historically accurate than the synoptic traditions.

In contemporary scholarship, this solution to the question of the
Gospel's historicity is no longer satisfying for several reasons. First, most
scholars now agree that the Gospel writers were not engaged in what we
typically expect from history-writing. In other words, none of the Gospel
writers understood their task to be writing an objective historical account
of the life of Jesus. Rather, the aim of their narratives was to tell a story
(the "good news," as the author of the Gospel of Mark calls it [Mark 1:1])
that communicated the meaning and significance of Jesus for the present
and future community of believers. As we will learn, they had different
sorts of resources on hand to craft these stories, some of which were likely
oral traditions transmitted from eyewitnesses, but others of which were
certainly traditional stories that developed in the creative imaginations of
Jesus's followers. Still other traditions about Jesus may well have emerged
in the creative imaginations of the Gospel writers. If we realize that the objective of the Gospel writers was to communicate what they understood to
be theological and christological truths about Jesus, rather than reporting
historical facts, we should not be overly troubled by this creativity. Indeed,
we should expect it from ancient followers of a revered figure.[2]

Clearly, all of this means we should be cautious about attributing
historicity to any particular encounter that the Johannine Jesus has with
other characters in the Gospel of John. Nevertheless, and this is the second point, the statement by Clement that John wrote a "spiritual gospel"
could be misleading if it leads to devaluing *any* historical aspects of the
Gospel of John while not perceiving the so-called spiritual aspects of the
Synoptic Gospels. To put it another way, *all* of the canonical Gospels concern spiritual matters. Every one of them communicates the christological
beliefs of early Jesus-followers. And all of the Gospels also are suspect in
terms of modern conceptions of facticity. Note, as an obvious example,
the very different "facts" about Jesus's birth that we find in the Gospels of
Matthew compared to Luke.

On the other hand, all four of the Gospels are related in some way
to the historical event of Jesus's ministry and crucifixion. Indeed, the

synoptic versions are not necessarily more historically accurate than the Gospel of John. The three-year span for Jesus's ministry in the Gospel of John, for example, seems more plausible than the one-year ministry presupposed in the Synoptic Gospels. It is difficult to image Jesus gaining enough of a following to attract the attention of Roman authorities in one year. The Gospel of John also provides a plausible reason for the Jewish authorities to fear Jesus's popularity. They are afraid that a growing moment around a political rival will bring Roman retaliation (see 1:49; 6:15; 11:48; 12:13-15).

For our purposes, we need not spend more time than this on the question of the historical accuracy of the Jesus traditions in the Gospel of John. In this book, we are primarily concerned with understanding the Gospel of John in its own historical context.[3] And, if there is one thing that all scholars agree on, it is that the Gospel of John was written at least five to seven decades after Jesus's earthly ministry. It is this period that has most interested historical critics of the Gospel.

So apart from the question of accuracy, what other types of historical questions are raised by the observations we outlined above? More than we have space to discuss here! In what follows, we enter a conversation about the Bible (including the Gospel of John) that has been unfolding since the seventeenth century. While we cannot follow all the threads of that conversation, we will begin with the type of question that preoccupied critics in the early stages of historical criticism. That will set the stage for studying the Gospel in light of the historical questions that have been at the center of late twentieth- and twenty-first-century Johannine scholarship.

Who Wrote the Gospel? Traditional Claims and Historical Analysis

Most introductions to the canonical Gospels devote a section to questions of who wrote the Gospel, when, and where. Let me be clear at the outset that it is not possible to simply report the answer to these questions. Such details are now lost to us, and the reality is that much of the rest of this chapter will dwell in the realm of theories and hypotheses about the origins of the Gospel. What we *can* report with certainty is the traditional answers to these questions.

First, a bit of background: You may have noticed that throughout this chapter, I have referred simply to "the author" of the Gospel. I have not referred to the author as "John," even though the writing is called the Gospel of John. There is a reason for this, though if you are entirely new to the academic study of the Gospels, it may come as a surprise. None of the four canonical Gospels, including the Gospel of John, identifies its author anywhere within the narrative. All four of the canonical Gospels were written anonymously and circulated that way until they were collected and put together in a single codex (the earliest form of book, as opposed to a scroll). Apparently, those responsible for these early narratives about Jesus felt no need to attach their names to their work. Why? Perhaps their goal was to offer an account of the "good news of Jesus" (as the author of Mark indicates [Mark 1:1]), rather than drawing attention to their own authority.

The need for designating a particular link to apostolic authority for each of these Gospels, including the Gospel of John, emerged in the second century CE when more gospels began to be written. These later gospels *did* claim the authority of those close to Jesus (for example, the Gospel of Philip, the Gospel of Mary, the Gospel of Thomas to name a few). In light of these associations, the titles or "superscriptions" were added to the collection of the four Gospels. This is why all of the Gospels have the same formula for their titles, "The Gospel according to…" In Greek, this is expressed with just one word, *kata*, placed before the traditional name, in our case *"kata Iōannān."* Note, however, that even these superscriptions do not necessarily imply that these figures actually *wrote* the respective Gospels, but only that the tradition is associated with these figures in some way.

But even once we have the title "according to John" as a superscription, those interested in trying to identify an author of the Gospel are still left with a puzzle. For one thing, the name "John" was as common in the first century as it is now. So who exactly is the John linked to this ancient Gospel? Our earliest evidence that claims that the disciple whom Jesus loved was John, that this John wrote the Gospel in Ephesus, comes from a second-century bishop named Irenaeus. Irenaeus wrote his most famous work, *Against the Heresies* (185 CE), to refute religious movements that he considered heretical and to assert the apostolic authority of what became the four canonical Gospels. In that context, he wrote, "Afterwards, John, the disciple of the Lord, who also had leaned upon His breast, did himself publish a Gospel during his residence at Ephesus in Asia" (3.1.1).

Until the beginning of biblical historical criticism, Irenaeus's statement about the Gospel's authorship was accepted as fact. But in the seventeenth century, scholars began to challenge this traditional claim. One basic problem is the fact that it is very unlikely that a disciple described in the Gospels as a Galilean fisherman would have the literacy skills necessary to write a Gospel narrative. In the ancient world, reading and writing at the level evident in the Gospel were typically limited to the elite class. Additionally, there are church traditions about the early martyrdom of John that are inconsistent with Irenaeus's claims (see, for instance, Mark 10:39; Matt 20:23).

Apart from the tradition from Irenaeus, the Gospel offers some tantalizing hints about the origin of at least some of its traditions. At 19:35, the narrator breaks into the narrative to address the audience: "He who saw this has testified so that you also may believe. His testimony is true, and he knows that he tells the truth." This assertion lends the authority of an eyewitness to the flow of blood and water that issues from Jesus's body after it is pierced by the Roman soldier's spear (19:34). This has led some to understand the entire Gospel as a tradition that stems from an eyewitness, most often linked to the "disciple whom Jesus loved" (typically referred to as the beloved disciple). But it is difficult to extend the claim to the rest of the Gospel since it includes scenes that could not have come from an eyewitness. What follower of Jesus would have witnessed Jesus's trial before Pilate in chapter 18, for example?

Another intriguing reference occurs at 21:24. Referring again to the beloved disciple, the writer states, "This is the disciple who is testifying to these things and has written them, and we know that his testimony is true." Here is a clear reference to writing, but a rather unclear reference to "these things." And who is the "we" who is now behind the writing? Or, for that matter, who is the "I" in the final verse who states, "But there are also many other things that Jesus did; if every one of them were written down, I suppose that the world itself could not contain the books that would be written (21:25)?

As you can see, the question of who wrote the Gospel is a complex and difficult one to answer, and it seems clear that the traditional answer of John, "the disciple whom Jesus loved," is not satisfactory on its own. Although there have been many hypotheses about the identity of this disciple, the fact is the Gospel does not identify the figure by name. If the point was to link the authorship of the Gospel to a *particular* historical figure, this is a strange way to do it.

Nor is it easy to assign a precise date to the composition of the Gospel. The standard answer has been to date its writing to the late first century CE, perhaps around 90 or 95 CE. Not only is the date suggested by Irenaeus's statement but it also is in keeping with most scholars' assumptions that John is the latest of the canonical Gospels. Because the Gospel of Mark is typically dated near the fall of the temple in 70 CE, and Luke and Matthew a decade or so later, John is assigned a date sometime soon after that. Additional support for the late-first-century date also appeared to come from the discovery of a papyrus fragment known as John Rylands papyrus 52. This small bit of papyrus contains verses from John 18. The initial publication of this fragment came with a tentative date of 130 CE and since then scholars have used it as the *terminus post quem*, that is, the latest date by which the Gospel could have been written. More recently, however, the method for dating this fragment has come under question, making its value for dating the Gospel less certain.[4]

In addition, it is not at all clear who, if any, of the earliest church theologians knew of the Gospel of John. The mid-second-century writings by Justin Martyr, for example, lack quotations or even direct allusions to the Gospel. This is true despite the fact this second-century writer (1) came to Rome from Ephesus and (2) wrote at length about Jesus as the *logos*. He does refer to a revelation coming from a man named John, but this is in connection with traditions from the book of Revelation (*Dialogue with Trypho*, 81). Another early church writer, Ignatius of Antioch, wrote a letter to the community in Ephesus in the second century in which he cites texts from the Pauline Letters, but nothing that is a direct quotation from the Gospel of John.[5] In short, as with identifying the author(s) of the Gospel of John, figuring precisely when it was completed has also proved elusive. In terms of location, Ephesus continues to be the most popular contender. Not only does church tradition situate it there, but another writing associated with the Johannine corpus, the book of Revelation, is clearly directed toward an audience in Asia Minor. Other suggestions for the Gospel's provenance include Palestine, Syria, and even Alexandria in Egypt.

The Question of Sources for the Gospel

Along with asking who wrote the Gospel, when, and where, historical critics have also been interested in the "how" question, or perhaps better, "using what sources?" Possible answers to this question include the incorporation of earlier written or oral sources known by the author but not by the authors of the Synoptic Gospels. Another possibility is that the Fourth Gospel uses the Synoptic Gospels themselves as sources.

In terms of the first possibility, Rudolf Bultmann posited multiple sources behind the Gospel, including, most famously, a "signs source" (Greek, *semeia* source). Evidence for a signs source is seen in the way the Gospel refers to a "first" and "second sign" as though from a written collection of signs (2:11; 4:54). Especially as the Gospel also refers to "many signs" before the reference to the "second" sign, it seems that another source may have been incorporated. From Bultmann's perspective, the use of a distinct signs source would also explain the tension between the Gospel's positive assessment of signs that he thought belonged to the source, and the more critical attitude toward signs also evident in the Gospel (see 4:48, cp. 20:29). Bultmann's source and composition theories set the stage for discussions of the formation of the Gospel well into the twentieth century.

The Gospel's relationship to the Synoptic Gospels has also been a central focus of source criticism, and conclusions about this relationship have shifted repeatedly over the years. Generally, three main options have been considered: (1) The author did not know the Synoptic Gospels and thus wrote independently. The shared traditions such as the feeding of the multitude are attributed to the author's knowledge of synoptic-like oral traditions. (2) The author knew and drew on at least some of the Gospels (Mark and Luke as primary candidates) in a limited fashion to write his Gospel. In this case, the Gospel writer is seen as responding to and recasting particular synoptic traditions to suit his own purposes. (3) John knew at least some of the Gospels, but did not use them as sources.

Because the details of each of these positions are too much to include here, I will simply point to places where one might see the author interacting with the synoptic traditions. The first place involves a scene with Jesus and the disciples just before his arrest. In the Gospel of Mark, this episode takes place in the garden of Gethsemane. Here is how the scene is narrated in Mark 14:32-36:

> They went to a place called Gethsemane; and he said to his disciples, "Sit here while I pray." He took with him Peter and James and John, and began to be distressed and agitated. And he said to them, "I am deeply grieved, even to death; remain here, and keep awake." And going a little farther, he threw himself on the ground and prayed that, if it were possible, the hour might pass from him. He said, "Abba, Father, for you all things are possible; remove this cup from me; yet, not what I want, but what you want."

The Markan Jesus then returns to find his disciples all asleep. In the Gospel of John, there is no such scene of distress in a garden. Instead, at 12:27 with no specific location mentioned the Johannine Jesus indicates that his soul is "troubled." But then he immediately poses a question:

> "And what should I say—'Father, save me from this hour'? No, it is for this reason that I have come to this hour. Father, glorify your name." Then a voice came from heaven, "I have glorified it, and I will glorify it again." (12:27-28)

One could see this version as a sort of "anti-Gethsemane" scene countering the Markan tradition that features Jesus's anguish and lack of enthusiasm about his imminent suffering. The case for the author's knowledge of the Gospel of Mark seems even stronger given what precedes this statement in John's Gospel, where the Johannine Jesus offers what appears to be the Johannine version of the Markan Jesus's teaching on discipleship. Compare these two statements:

> For those who want to save their life will lose it, and those who lose their life for my sake, and for the sake of the gospel, will save it. (Mark 8:35)

> Those who love their life will lose it, and those who hate their life in this world will keep it for eternal life. (John 12:25)

Note the distinctively Johannine use of the love/hate contrast, the reference to life in "this world," and the reward of "eternal life" in what otherwise are parallel teachings.

The Gospel of John also shares some striking overlaps with material that is unique to the Gospel of Luke among the Synoptic Gospels. For example, only John and Luke mention Martha and Mary (Luke 10:38-42 / John 11:1-44). Only these two Gospels have a character named Lazarus (Luke 16:19-31 / John 11:1-44). Both of them also feature Peter running to the empty tomb, although in the Gospel of John, he is accompanied by the disciple whom Jesus loved (Luke 12:24 / John 20:3-4).

Still, these examples do not provide decisive evidence that the Gospel writer had written versions of the Synoptic Gospels. Some argue that the author of John knew only oral traditions that were similar to what we read in Mark and Luke. In any case, it is easy to see why scholars differ in their theories about the relationship between John and the Synoptic Gospels.

Multiple Authors and the History "behind" the Gospel

As is evident from this discussion of authorship, most scholars now recognize that imagining a single author penning the entire Gospel of John does not make adequate sense of the textual evidence, let alone one of his disciples (e.g., John). The story is not narrated from the perspective of a particular disciple, and there are many scenes that are narrated where no disciples are present. Again, one might consider who the eyewitness could have been for Jesus's trial before Pilate in chapter 19. Or who could have observed the interrogations between the man born blind and the Pharisees in chapter 9? As we will see in the next chapter, both of these scenes have the mark of dramatic development indicating the author's literary skill more than an eyewitness account.

Indeed, many aspects of the Gospel point to a text that expanded over time perhaps under multiple authorial hands. This reading of the evidence shifts the focus of historical analysis from speculation about the identity of "an" author to attempts to reconstruct the particular series of historical events that would explain this layered composition. As we will see, in the mid to late twentieth century, this is precisely the direction taken by scholars of the Gospel. But this new reading of the evidence was not simply the next intellectual step taken in deliberations about events in the first century CE. It was also motivated by tragic events in the twentieth century. Let's turn again to the Gospel to understand the emergence of this new direction in its historical interpretation.

Consider the following elements of the Gospel narrative. The Johannine Jesus goes several times to Jerusalem to attend Jewish festivals. We have already noted the reference to three Passover festivals (2:23; 6:4; 13:1). In addition, Jesus goes to an unspecified festival at 5:1, and he is in Jerusalem for the festival of the Booths in 7:2-14 (in spite of telling his disciples he will not attend). Not only does Jesus attend Jewish festivals, he is regularly compared to Jewish ancestors, for example, Abraham (8:52-58), Jacob (4:12-14), and Moses (e.g., 1:17; 3:14). Finally, in his conversation with a woman from Samaria, Jesus declares that salvation is from the Jews (4:22).

In the mix of these associations between Jesus and Judaism, we read also of repeated conflictual encounters with opponents designated as "the Jews." Scholars often use quotation marks around this phrase to signal that there is something problematic in this translation. In fact, a major question for historical criticism of the Gospel is who or what is meant by the Greek term behind this phrase, *hoi Iudaioi*.

As we saw in our initial reading, this group appears to be in regular conflict with Jesus. Early in the Gospel, we read of "the Jews" sending "priests and Levites from Jerusalem" to question John about his identity (1:19). A few verses later, we read that questioners were sent by the Pharisees (1:24).

In chapter 2, "the Jews" ask Jesus for a sign to explain his disruptive actions in the temple. In chapter 5, the paralytic healed by Jesus informs "the Jews" that it was Jesus who had healed him on the Sabbath so that they begin to persecute him (5:15-16), and soon seek to kill him (5:18). More than once, "the Jews" try to stone Jesus (8:59; 10:31). As we noted in the last chapter, the anti-Jewish language of the Gospel reaches a climax in John 8 where Jesus argues "the Jews" are children of the devil, not of Abraham nor of God (8:39-44). In short, the Gospel repeatedly points to a conflictual relationship between Jesus and "the Jews." Moreover, "the Jews" also cause fear in others so that no one will speak openly about Jesus (7:13). In two places the narrator suggests this fear is due to threats of being cast out of the synagogue (*aposynagogos*, 9:22; 12:42). The Johannine Jesus also predicts this will happen to his followers after his departure (16:2).

The problem is that historically Jesus and his disciples were all Jewish. How is it that the Gospel writer could portray Jesus as speaking of "your law" as if the Torah was not also his law? Given his own Jewish identity, how could the Johannine Jesus refer in this often oppositional way to the Jewish people in general? Here we might note that in the Synoptic Gospels, Jesus engages in conflict with groups designated as Pharisees, scribes, Sadducees, but never "the Jews." These groups are also mentioned in John, but they seem to be interchangeable with "the Jews."

To put it another way, scholars wonder what historical circumstances would motivate the Gospel writer to tell the story of Jesus using this phrase to designate the opponents of Jesus. This set of questions developed with pointed urgency in the wake of the horrific genocide of Jewish people during WWII. The tragic reality is that the anti-Jewish rhetoric of the Gospels, most clearly illustrated in the Gospel of John, helped contribute to the deaths of millions of Jews. Indeed, after a long history of persecution of Jews by Christians, scholars felt compelled to acknowledge and examine the anti-Jewish rhetoric of the Gospel more deeply.[6]

Reading the Gospel through the Synagogue-Expulsion Paradigm

In 1968, J. Louis Martyn wrote a small volume titled *History and Theology of the Fourth Gospel*. The first question of the Gospel that Martyn poses in the introduction to his book is "why should the Johannine Jesus, himself a Jew, engage in such an intensely hostile exchange with 'the Jews'?"[7] The question is especially pressing in light of Jesus's statement to the Samaritan woman in chapter 4 that "salvation is from the Jews."[8] With this question, the stage was set for a reorientation in Johannine studies.

Before Martyn's publication, most scholars followed Bultmann in viewing the conceptual background of the Gospel to be an early pre-Christian form of Gnosticism. The term *Gnosticism* (from *gnosis*, the Greek word for knowledge) is an umbrella term used to describe a number of movements and their accompanying writings that emerged in the second century CE that focused on attaining special knowledge as a key to transcendent existence, that is, salvation from the material world.[9] Since Martyn's work, most historical scholarship on the Gospel has assumed that the Gospel grew out of a local Jewish synagogue milieu, although the nature of the relationship to the local synagogue remains a point of debate.

So what was Martyn's influential theory? He proposed that the Gospel is best understood as "a two-level drama." On one level, the Gospel tells the story of Jesus. On another level, the Gospel relates the traumatic events of a particular community of believers that occurred decades after the death of Jesus. In other words, Martyn suggested that the writer of the Gospel related events that occurred in his own community by means of the story of Jesus. At times, the second level, the community's story, bubbles to the surface and breaks out into the first level, the story of Jesus, in a clear way. Martyn argues that this is what happens in chapter 9 with the story of the man born blind. A crucial verse for this theory is John 9:22: "His parents said this because they were afraid of the Jews; for the Jews had already agreed that anyone who confessed Jesus to be the Messiah would be put out of the synagogue."

The Greek word used to express "expelled from the synagogue" (*aposynagōgos*) appears nowhere else in the New Testament or early Christian literature. Martyn argued that it relates to a formal decision instituted by Jewish authorities that could not have existed during the lifetime of Jesus. In addition, he suggested that the "agreement" of 9:22 referred to a post-70 CE addition of a "curse against the heretics" to a daily synagogue prayer. The theory was that if one could not publicly recite the *Birkhat ha-minim*, which presumably was directed toward followers of Jesus, one would suffer expulsion from the synagogue.

Martyn's synagogue expulsion theory soon became the primary basis for late–twentieth-century historical reconstructions of a particular community that was responsible for producing the Johannine literature. Whereas earlier historical studies of the Gospel explained the presence of textual breaks and inconsistencies as due to the combination and editing of various sources, this same data was now explained in a different way. While the possibility of different sources was still acknowledged, more focus was directed to what the Johannine literature revealed about the trials and tribulations of what came to be called "the Johannine community."[10] The approach is clearly seen in the title of a book by Raymond Brown, *The Community of the Beloved Disciple: The Life, Love and Hates on an Individual Church in New Testament Times*.[11] In fact, Brown became a leading voice in the reconstruction of the Johannine community.

Brown drew on the work of Martyn to reconstruct four different phases of the Johannine community that corresponded to different layers of composition of the Johannine literature. He develops these phrases in detail in *The Community of the Beloved Disciple*. In brief, his four phases of development include:

1) **The origins of the community.** The stage before the Gospel was written during which several different groups in or near Palestine accept Jesus as the messiah (for example, Jews with standard messianic expectations including followers of John the Baptist and converts from Samaria). This was a time of self-definition of the community in light of other groups.

2) **The Gospel-writing phase.** This is a period of intra-community conflict. The rejection of Johannine Christology by Jewish Christians convinces the Johannine community that the world is opposed to Jesus. As the Gospel is written, the community assumes an increasingly strong stance against those it determines to be nonbelievers.

3) **The epistle-writing phase.** The community begins to experience internal divisions. The Letters show a more conservative approach than the Gospel in areas such as Christology (see chapter 4 of this book). This approach brings the community closer toward the "greater church."

4) **The post-epistle phase**—dissolution of a distinct Johannine group and union with the "great church." The Johannine community comes under the official teaching of the bishops.

The work of Martyn and Brown has had enormous and ongoing influence on how scholars think about history behind the Gospel of John. Even if many scholars question the details of their proposals, the notion of a "Johannine community" is now a mainstay in much scholarship on the Johannine literature.

Objections to the Synagogue Expulsion Theory

Nevertheless, not everyone has been convinced that the scenario of Jesus-believers being expelled from the Jewish synagogue is the key to unlocking the puzzles of the Gospel of John. In fact, despite the enormous popularity of this historical reconstruction among Johannine scholars in the second half of the twentieth century, there have been serious objections to several of its underlying premises. The following are the major objections to the theory, which include both external evidence regarding status of rabbinic Judaism in the first and second centuries CE and internal evidence from the Gospel and Epistles.

1) As many now concede, there is no evidence that the *Benediction against the Heretics* was added to the synagogue prayer in the first or even second century CE. It is uncertain when exactly the curse was introduced, since any firm evidence for its use dates only to the late fourth century. Even if the curse was introduced earlier, the term "minim" is nonspecific and likely did not specifically target Jesus-followers. In fact, there is evidence that some Christians were still participating in the synagogue as late as the fourth century.[12] This hardly suggests that synagogue leaders were in the

business of expelling Christians. Rather the concern seems to be that Christians are attracted to worship in the synagogue.

2) There is no evidence that rabbinic leaders would have had the type of power assumed by the expulsion theory. Recent work has demonstrated that in the first and second centuries, rabbis were a small group in survival mode, following the destruction of the Jerusalem temple. They were not effecting policy in synagogues across the Roman Empire.[13]

3) Even though there are references to being cast out of the synagogue in the Gospel, it is hardly a major theme in the Gospel. Critics of the theory argue that these few references have been given far too much precedence vis-à-vis the major themes of the Gospel.

4) In addition to the expulsion passages, there are other references to the Jews in the Gospel that are at least neutral if not positive. For example, Martha and Mary are supported by the Jews who mourn with them when Lazarus dies. And, as we have seen, the festivals of the Jews are regularly attended by Jesus.

5) There is evidence from this period that points to hostility flowing in the other direction—that is from Jesus-believers against non-believers. Certainly, the vitriolic language of John 8 suggests animus toward the group represented with the term "the Jews."

Alternative Proposals to the Synagogue Expulsion Hypothesis

One argument against Martyn's expulsion hypothesis is a wholesale rejection of the idea of a particular Johannine community. Richard Bauckham challenges the idea that the canonical Gospels, including the Gospel of John, were written with specific communities in mind.[14] He argues that a local community would have no need to have traditions written down because oral communication would suffice. Written texts were used in the ancient world to spread ideas to distant readers. From Bauckham's perspective, the very fact that gospels were written, and especially that they were written in codex form (that is, in the more portable book form rather than on scrolls) indicates that they were intended for dissemination to a wide audience.

While Bauckham is right to question the elaborate hypothetical reconstructions of gospel communities, the fact that there are also three letters that share the conceptual world of the Gospel of John adds weight to the idea of there being some circle of believers associated with this literature. Moreover, Bauckham's overall project is to argue for traditional claims of the Gospels as based on eyewitness accounts. But, arguing that the Gospel is based on eyewitness accounts simply returns us to the historical problems that we discussed earlier about this traditional claim about authorship.

Adele Reinhartz offers another theory for explaining the "*aposynagogus*" language in the Gospel. Perhaps the issue is that a group of Jesus-believers were *opting* out of the synagogue, rather than being expelled from it. Here she notes the reference to deserting in 12:11, where it states that because of Jesus's raising of Lazarus from the dead, many of the Jews were deserting and were believing in Jesus. It is possible that this detail is more historically accurate than the references to being cast out of the synagogue. Note that the three uses of *aposynagogos* do not actually report this event occurring. In the first case, it is referred to as a threat (9:22), in the second case as a fear (12:42), and in the third case as a future possibility (16:2). Thus, Reinhartz proposes that these references may have been a rhetorical strategy to discourage those who had departed the synagogue from returning to it.[15]

As I mentioned, in spite of these serious objections and the lack of external evidence in support of the synagogue expulsion theory, it remains deeply ingrained in historical scholarship of the Gospel.

Socio-Historical and Social-Identity Approaches to the Gospel of John

Another way of thinking about the historical situation of the Gospel comes from analyzing it with the use of social-science theories. The first scholar to do this was Wayne Meeks. In 1972 Meeks published an article titled "The Man from Heaven in Johannine Sectarianism," which built on Martyn's historical reconstruction, but with a sociological dimension added to the analysis.[16] Meeks was especially interested in the following question: What does religious language and practice *do* for people? With respect to the Gospel of John, he asked what its particular linguistic formulations do for the Johannine community. Further, he wanted to know what *type* of community would produce the sort of language found in the Gospel. By this Meeks meant the dualistic language that we noticed in the last chapter, and the way that Jesus is presented as an enigmatic figure sent from above.

As his title suggests, Meeks thought the dualistic language of the Gospel told a story of Jesus as a "stranger from heaven" and that this story reflected the sense of alienation that the Johannine group experienced as it separated itself from "the world." At the same time, the dualistic language functioned to bolster the group's identity. Using sociological categories, Meeks defined the Johannine community as sectarian. It was a group set apart not only from the Jewish synagogue but also from other expressions of early Christianity. The effect of his work was to further solidify the expulsion hypothesis and to open debate on the precise sociological nature of the Johannine community. Although not everyone has been convinced that "sect" is the best term for the Johannine group, scholars have followed Meeks's lead in drawing on social scientific approaches to learn more about the Gospel.[17]

More recently, for example, Raimo Hakola has suggested that we might better understand the Johannine language if we think of its function in creating (rather than reflecting) a particular group identity.[18] Consider the way that certain groups of friends or particular communities often feel more closely connected because they share a common way of thinking and talking about the world. Even more, consider the tendency of groups to secure their own identity by discriminating against another group. Social identity theorists study these types of human social behaviors, noting that individual actions are affected by interpersonal relationships and intergroup relationships. In other words, a person may behave one way when hanging out with one friend, another way when part of a larger group of friends, and yet a different way when meeting with a group of coworkers. Furthermore, social theorists observe that just the *perception* of belonging to a particular group triggers feelings of commitment to one's supposed "in-group" at the expense of others. That is, social groups tend to *manufacture* intergroup differences from other groups to distinguish themselves. They may also give special positive value to existing differences from others in order to build a sense of group cohesion.

Analyzing the Gospel through the lens of social identity theory opens new possibilities for understanding the Johannine language that expresses alienation from the world. Rather than reflecting a particular (possibly sectarian) community, Hakola suggests that the Gospel creates a symbolic world in which an "imagined community" can find its home. What is "imagined," according to Hakola, is not the community itself, but rather, the community's relationship to the rest of the world. The Johannine literature may have encouraged its intended reading community to perceive themselves as alienated from and victimized by the "world," even as its members went about their daily interactions with other Jews and Gentiles living in their locale. In so doing, the Gospel contributes to the project of defining an "in-group" that is separated from others in the perceived reality of its members, even if they are not actually alienated from those around them.

Reading the Gospel in Its Roman Imperial Context

As we have seen, late–twentieth-century study of the Gospel of John was preoccupied with questions of its Jewish context, especially trying to make sense of the repeated use of the term "the Jews" as a reference to Jesus's opponents. To be sure, in the wake of the catastrophic genocide of Jewish people during WWII, there was and still is good reason to probe the meaning and function of the term in the Gospel. But the nearly exclusive focus on understanding the so-called Johannine community and its relationship to the synagogue overlooked another pressing and well-established historical reality for the author and his audience: they all were living under Roman imperial rule. Whatever difficulties the audience of the Gospel might have had with the local synagogue (and this remains a point of debate), there is no doubt that daily life would have been shaped by imperial rule.

Attention to this historical reality has led to the emergence of an interpretive approach variously referred to as empire studies, empire-critical, or imperial-critical. The main goal of this approach is to read the Gospels as literature that reflects the complex ways that people negotiated life under foreign rule. To that end, with respect to the Gospel of John, empire studies seek a nuanced understanding of what life would have been like under first-century CE Roman rule in, say, Ephesus (the city commonly associated with the Gospel).

Warren Carter offers just such a detailed study in *John and Empire*.[19] To understand life under empire, he draws both on social-science models of empire, along with material and epigraphical evidence of the lived reality in ancient Ephesus.[20] Here I only highlight some basic differences between our first-world contemporary life and life in the first-century CE Mediterranean that should inform our reading of the Gospel in its Roman imperial context. The first is an absence of a sizable middle class in which one could expect to live a reasonably comfortable life. Instead, the provincial cities of the Roman Empire featured a small, wealthy elite class, as well as select group of professionals such as scribes, religious functionaries, soldiers, administrators, and slaves who supported the elites. Beyond these elites and their "retainers," the vast majority of the population struggled to live at or often below subsistence levels. The Roman Empire developed a multi-pronged approach to maintaining and controlling this social system, which ranged from brute military force to the promulgation of a Roman imperial theology that assured the world of the peace and order brought by the divinely empowered Roman rule.[21]

We have already seen some evidence against the synagogue-expulsion theory for the historical setting of the Gospel. Carter adds to that evidence by pointing to the ways that diaspora synagogues (synagogues outside of Palestine) were typically integrated into the broader civic life. Synagogues were not simply concerned with "religion" and "religious" disputes. Indeed, this is an important reminder for all of our thinking about the ancient world. Religious practice in the ancient world was primarily a cultic practice that pertained to certain civic responsibilities. As such, these cultic activities were intricately interwoven with multiple aspects of social life—political, economic, cultural, and so on. An empire critical approach keeps this web of connections in view.

As a result, there are some explicit ways that we see the Gospel reflecting its place in the Roman imperial world. As I mentioned earlier, only this Gospel openly acknowledges a threat from Rome. Following the raising of Lazarus by Jesus, the Jewish council worries about a growing number of followers. They remark, "If we let him go on like this, everyone will believe in him, and the Romans will come and destroy both our holy place and our nation" (11:48). One might also wonder whether John 12:31 alludes to the Roman emperor with its claims that, "Now the ruler of this world will be driven out." Certainly, the status of Roman power is challenged by Jesus during his trial before Pilate. There Jesus boldly asserts that Pilate has no power other than what God allows him to have (19:10-11).

There are additional less-explicit ways that the Gospel offers evidence of engagement and negotiation with its imperial context. Carter argues that the Gospel writer offers a "rhetoric of distance" to discourage what he posits as an over-accommodation to Roman imperial power. In this reading, the Gospel's in-group language may not reflect sectarianism, as much as the promotion of a particular stance vis-à-vis the (Roman) world. Here are three examples that Carter offers as evidence of how the Gospel urges differentiation rather than engagement with imperial rule. In each case, the point is to show how the Gospel writer draws or responds to rhetorical strategies that were commonly used to establish authority and power in order to promote an alternative view of the cosmic order.

1) **The turn to the past.** In the Greco-Roman period, writers and orators frequently drew on past authorities to legitimize their own claims to power. This is true also of the Gospel writers who situate the work of Jesus in relation to past figures such as Moses, Abraham, and the prophets. Carter notes that in the Gospel of John, Jesus and his opponents both claim the authority of these ancestors (see, for example, 3:14; 4:12; 5:45-46; 8:52-58). Ultimately,

the Johannine Jesus is associated with a time that existed even
before these authorial figures (e.g., 1:1; 8:58).

2) **Images and titles for Jesus.** Both "savior" and "son of God" were
titles used in relation to the emperor. They are not titles that are
regularly used for God in the Hebrew scriptures. Carter suggests
that their application to Jesus is a way of contesting the power
and authority of the emperor, and redirecting such claims to
power toward Jesus.[22]

3) **Eschatological Promises from the Roman Empire versus from
the Gospel.** The Roman Empire promised to bring a golden
age of peace and prosperity, often by way of their poets. Vergil's
Aeneid predicts the indefinite closing of the gates of war under
Augustus, and his Fourth *Eclogue* envisions a reign of peace and
abundance. What would the Johannine Jesus's promises to the
believer of an "eternal life" that is somehow already present mean
to his audience alongside this Roman imperial eschatology? One
thing that would be clear to the vast majority of people living
during this time was that they were not living in a golden age of
abundance. As noted above, the material reality of daily life in the
first and second centuries CE was difficult at best. Carter argues
the Gospel evokes eschatological traditions that "expose and
conflict with the norms and claims of elite imperial practices and
propaganda" and speak to the injustice of Roman rule for most
people.[23] Moreover, he suggests that the emphasis on abundance
that comes from Jesus's signs is a response to the privation that
was a regular part of life.

Much more could be said about the Gospel of John from a historical
perspective, at least in terms of the long history of debate about these major topics. My goal here has been to introduce you to the major problems
and persistent historical questions about the Gospel and the group that
was responsible for its composition. Along the way, I hope also to have
alerted you to some of the limits of historical reconstruction. Indeed, it
was the recognition of those limits that led, in part, to another approach
to the study of the Gospel, which we turn to in the next chapter.

Chapter 3

Exploring Literary Design
in the Gospel of John

In the last chapter, we explored historical questions such as how, when, and by whom the Gospel was written. These types of questions concern the world *behind* the text. This chapter will focus on the Gospel's literary features or the *world in the text*, often called the story-world. To focus on this story-world, we will combine two different ways that scholars have studied the literary aspects of the Gospel. The first approach draws on literary-critical methods that grew out of departments of English literature in the twentieth century. The second approach examines how consideration of the Gospel alongside other ancient literary genres aids in our interpretation. A brief overview of each type of literary approach will be useful for the discussion that follows.

As we saw in the last chapter, historical critical investigation shaped the sort of questions that scholars asked of the Gospel for most of the nineteenth and twentieth centuries. However, late in the twentieth century, some scholars began to ask new types of questions. Rather than focusing on a hypothetical history of a Johannine community and treating the Gospel as if it were a mirror reflecting events in the life of this community, they focused on the text in its final form as a literary work. R. Alan Culpepper, who was the first to use contemporary literary theories for a sustained analysis of the Gospel, describes his literary critical study of the Gospel as follows: "Our aim is to contribute to understanding the gospel as a narrative text, what it is, and how it works. The emphasis will be upon analysis and interpretation rather than upon the construction of hypotheses or critique of methods."[1] In this way, Culpepper clearly distinguishes a literary approach from the historical-critical method we explored in the last chapter. In this chapter then, we will examine how the Gospel works as a story, discussing narrative elements such as plot, characters, and literary devices.

Yet, there are limitations to a literary-critical approach that removes the Gospel completely from its historical context. After all, it is an ancient text, centuries removed from the modern novels that literary critics often analyze. For this reason, good literary analysis must include a historical dimension. But rather than reconstructing particular events or a history of a community behind the Gospel, adding a historical dimension to a literary-critical approach involves comparing the Gospel with other ancient literary genres. It means asking, what *type* of work did the author(s) think they were writing, and what literary conventions of their time were used to convey meaning?

Consider the fact that all authors must use literary conventions to communicate their ideas. Even as I write this book, I'm drawing on certain literary conventions that are typical for an introductory textbook—explanatory subheadings, endnotes, questions for the reader to consider, and so on. So also, the Gospel writer had a range of literary conventions that guided his composition. At a broad level, the Gospel shares much in common with other ancient biographies. The biography was a common type of literature in the Greco-Roman world, one focused on presenting a person for praise and emulation. Richard Burridge has convincingly shown how the Gospel of John features many of the same topics that were common to biographies of philosophers and teachers.[2] Such biographies often described the actions and teachings of a charismatic figure, and narrated details such as their ancestry, birth, education, great deeds, virtues, and death. Beyond this general classification, comparisons at a more narrow level show that the Gospel writer drew freely on conventions from Greek drama and perhaps even the ancient Greek romance novels. In fact, the way the Gospel writer works across different genres has led some to see the Gospel as a "genre mosaic."[3]

This chapter's literary approach to the Gospel will include these two types of analysis. We will study the basic literary elements of the Gospel, its plot, characters, and certain literary devices like the use of irony. But we will also situate these elements in their ancient literary setting, in particular seeing how the Gospel writer drew on conventions of Greek drama.

The Johannine Plot

Think about the Whole Story

Take time to reflect on the entire narrative of the Gospel. What are the main events of the narrative? What is it that makes the story move forward? Hint: remember the discussion in the first chapter of this book about the Prologue (1:1-18) offering an overview of the Gospel.

If it is true that the Gospel is a type of ancient biography, we should expect it to begin with attention to Jesus's origins and early life. The Gospels of Matthew and Luke do just this with their opening birth narratives (Matt 1–2; Luke 1–2). Seen in this light, the Prologue of the Gospel does provide information of Jesus's origins, even if it is not a story of Jesus's birth and early childhood. Instead, the origins story in the Prologue alerts the audience to the fact that the biography of the man Jesus is part of a cosmic story of the *logos* that begins outside of historical time and space. As Adele Reinhartz puts it, the Prologue introduces a "cosmological tale" that provides a reading guide for interpreting the "historical tale" of the life of Jesus.[4] In particular, this cosmological tale helps the audience make sense of the various temporal and spatial references that occur in the historical tale of Jesus. So, for example, when Jesus refers to his earlier existence (e.g., 8:58), the fact that the Prologue's reference to a cosmological "beginning" serves as an interpretive key. Similarly, when he speaks of his origin from above (8:23), the Prologue's description of the Word coming into the world (1:9, 14) allows the reader to understand what he means. And when Jesus says he is returning to the Father (e.g., 17:11; 20:17) the intimacy expressed between Jesus and the Father spoken of in 1:18 provides a structure for understanding this language.[5]

There is yet another dimension of the Gospel's plot signaled by the last verse of the Prologue, 1:18. Kasper Bro Larsen argues that the first half of the verse—"No one has ever seen God"—expresses a basic premise of the Gospel. He notes that, from a religious perspective, this is the problem of the human condition in general—the fundamental hiddenness of the divine from human beings. Given this premise, the second half of John 1:18 offers a response—"It is God the only Son, who is close to the Father's heart, who has made him known." Thus, according to Larsen, the Gospel's fundamental claim is that "the Son has overcome the cognitive distance between God and [humans] and enabled religious knowledge."[6] Larsen calls this aspect the "epistemological plot" of the Gospel. By this he means that the plot involves a series of scenes that reflect knowing and not knowing, or as we will discuss further below, recognition and non-recognition of the true identity of Jesus. The importance of this cognitive dimension of the plot is highlighted in 20:31, which features "coming to belief" as the very purpose of the narrative: "these [signs] are written so that you may come to believe that Jesus is the Messiah, the Son of God, and that through believing you may have life in his name."

The Divinity of Jesus

The reference to the "divinity" of Jesus here and in other places in the book should be read in light of the historical context of the Gospel. While we are not certain exactly when the Gospel was written, we know that it reached its final form well before the christological debates of the fourth century CE. This means that Christian doctrines about Christ did not yet exist. Theologians had not yet debated about the divine and human nature of the person of Jesus or about the triune nature of God. In fact, the Gospel of John helped fuel later christological debates with its paradoxical assertions about Jesus. We will return to this issue in chapter 4.

Related to this epistemological, or "knowing," aspect of the narrative, is the theme of conflict and division that occurs when the incarnate Word enters the finite world. This conflict is initially expressed in symbolic terms as a struggle between the forces of light and those of darkness (1:3-9). It is then stated in more concrete terms. Some people reject "the light" while others accept it/him (1:10-14). In this way, the Prologue points to a tragic element that will run through the narrative: although the world came to being through the light/Jesus, it did not recognize him. Moreover, those who rejected Jesus were "his own" (1:11). On the other hand, the audience is informed of the reward for those who believed: newly born, they received power to become children of God (1:12-13). The momentary shift to first-person plural in verse 14, "we have seen his glory," suggests a group that is testifying to the reality of this experience.

As we move into the narrative proper, the competing movements of the mission of the Word in the world and the world's opposition (or blindness) to this mission drive the plot forward. In other words, like most good narratives, the story depends on the conflict between the protagonist and an antagonist. In this case, the protagonist is Jesus whose purpose is to make his Father known (e.g., 1:18; 10:38; 14:7). His opponents are those who, according to the narrative, do not know God and thus attempt to thwart him (8:19, 54-55).[7]

Notably, the opponents appear in the story before Jesus does. The first scene after the Prologue features a group sent by "the Jews" in Jerusalem to question John, the one sent by God to witness to Jesus (1:19). Then, an even more direct conflict emerges between "the Jews" in Jerusalem and Jesus himself. In chapter 2, the Johannine Jesus travels to Jerusalem and violently disrupts the temple practices (2:13-16). The Jews understandably ask for an explanation, and Jesus's puzzling response in 2:19, "Destroy this temple, and in three days I will raise it up," hardly satisfies their request. Something similar happens in 5:15. Jesus's opponents interpret a healing he performs as a violation of the prohibition to work on the Sabbath. When Jesus defends his actions, he does so in a provocative way, so that they seek "all the more to kill him" (5:17-18). From this point on, the Gospel features reminders of the threat against Jesus's life at regular intervals (7:1; 11:53; 12:10).

Meanwhile, alongside these deadly threats are regular reminders of the cosmological tale. The Johannine Jesus insists that he is the one in control of his life and death. As we saw at the temple scene, the narrator explains that his confusing response refers to Jesus raising up his own body from the dead (2:19). In chapter 10, the Johannine Jesus speaks in ways that reflect the plot's cosmic dimensions. Speaking of how he lays down his life for his sheep, the Johannine Jesus asserts: "For this reason the Father loves me, because I lay down my life in order to take it up again. No one takes it from me, but I lay it down of my own accord. I have power to lay it down, and I have power to take it up again. I have received this command from my Father" (10:17-18).

Sometimes this cosmic storyline breaks into the flow of the earthly one. This occurs, for example, in the arrest scene in chapter 18. There, with the assistance of Judas (who acts as an agent of Satan [13:27]), the Jewish authorities send soldiers and police to arrest Jesus (the one who acts as the agent of God).[8] But here Jesus momentarily assumes control of the scene—he interrogates the soldiers (twice). Then, when he identifies himself with the statement "I am he" (Gk. *ego eimi*), they fall to the ground before him (18:4-6). This is a strange response for the earthly tale unless one realizes that Jesus's words, which can also be translated "I am," echo passages in the Hebrew Bible that use the same phrase for God (Isa 43:10, 25; see also Exod 3:14). This episode reminds the audience of the power of Jesus and God's cosmic plan for him just at the point where scenes of Jesus's trial, torture, and crucifixion are about to begin.

Most contemporary discussions of plot suggest that plots have a climactic point toward which the action builds. Given the presence of the cosmological and historical tales, as well as the epistemological plot that is present in the narrative, can we identify such a high point in the Gospel? This is a difficult question for several reasons. First, unlike the experience of reading a modern novel, the Gospel writer assumes the audience knows how the story will end. There are no real surprises for the Gospel's intended audience as the narrative progresses. Second, whereas one might consider the resurrection scenes at the end of the Gospel as the sign of the Johannine Jesus's ultimate triumph over his opposition, throughout the narrative he has spoken of his *death* as the moment of glorification. The repeated references to Jesus's coming "hour" refer both to his death and to his glorification (2:4; 7:30; 8:20; 12:23, 27; 13:1; 16:25, 32; 17:1).

Rather than look for a single high point of the narrative, some have argued that the Gospel depicts Jesus moving episodically though a journey of descent and ascent. The beginning of this journey is announced with the description of the *logos* coming into the world (1:9). That this is imagined as a descent is clear when Jesus later describes himself as the "one who descended from heaven" (3:13). About midway through the Gospel, the narrator indicates a shift from this descent toward Jesus's ascent to the Father. At this point, the narrator reports that Jesus knew that the hour to "go to the Father" had arrived (13:1).[9] Then toward the end of the narrative the Johannine Jesus's words to Mary Magdalene signal the impending completion of this journey. He instructs her to "go to my brothers and say to them, 'I am ascending to my Father and your Father, to my God and your God'" (20:17).[10]

In addition to seeing this journey of descent and ascent of the *logos*, we can learn about how the Johannine plot works by attending to the author's use of recognition scenes where moments of "discovery" (*anagnorisis* in Greek) occur. Such scenes were a common plot device in ancient Greek drama. Aristotle describes them as follows: "*Anagnorisis* is, as the very word implies, a change from ignorance to knowledge, and thus to either love or hate, in the personages marked for good or evil fortune" (*Poetics* 10.1-2). An important element of the recognition scene is the effect of such scenes on the audience. Those who have full knowledge of the hidden identity of the unrecognized character are able to enjoy the interplay between the characters as well as the suspense that builds between what seems to be and what actually is.

A number of scholars have made significant contributions to our understanding of the Gospel based on the use of recognition scenes. According to Larsen, the typical recognition scene in ancient literature includes some form of the following elements:[11]

1. The meeting—a meeting between the observer and the observed

2. The move of cognitive resistance—the observer typically reacts first with lack of recognition regarding the identity of the observed.

3. The display of a token—the observed shows a token, creating a turning point in the scene. This move may lead to recognition, or to further resistance.

4. The moment of recognition—identification of the observed with a proper name or a thematic role.

5. Report of emotional reactions of and physical contact following the moment of recognition

There are many examples of such moments of recognition in Greek drama and narrative. A premier example comes from Euripides's *The Bacchae*. In this Greek tragedy, the god Dionysus disguises himself as a human being before coming to the kingdom of Thebes. He seeks vengeance for slander and intends to demonstrate that he was born a god. The audience watches as the unrecognized god uses riddles and double meanings in his encounter with Pentheus to lead the king to his demise. Scholars have seen many parallels between the Gospel and this tragedy suggesting the author was familiar with the tragic genre, including the use of recognition scenes.[12]

Another classical recognition scene occurs in Homer's *Odyssey*. Late in the epic, Odysseus finally returns home from a twenty-year absence but he is disguised by the goddess Athena as an old beggar. As his childhood nurse bathes his feet, she sees and touches a scar on Odysseus's leg leftover from a childhood wound. The recognition of the scar brings about a recognition of Odysseus. The presentation of the mark or token that enables recognition is a regular feature of *anagnorisis*. In the Gospel of John, Thomas recognizes Jesus after being encouraged to see and touch Jesus's wounds (20:27-28). The Gospel depicts another such moment of recognition just a few verses earlier when Mary Magdalene first mistakes the risen Jesus for the gardener. It is only when Jesus calls her by name that she recognizes him (20:11-16).

Although these two scenes occur toward the end of the Gospel, such moments of recognition occur early and throughout the Gospel. As we have seen, the Prologue sets the condition for recognizing who Jesus is—the true light, the incarnate *logos* that exists as a cocreator with God. Thus, as Larsen argues, with the Johannine recognition scenes the recognition of Jesus's proper name is not the main goal, but rather recognition of the mark of his divinity.[13] So, for example, Thomas does not cry out "Jesus!" when he realizes who he is with but rather "My Lord and my God!" (20:28). In this sense, the moments of recognition serve as a bridge between the historical tale, the story of Jesus's early life, and the tale of his cosmic origins and divine identity. As Larsen notes, the scenes are also part of the Gospel's epistemological plot because they concern the gaining of knowledge or belief. Finally, because it is the characters in the Gospel who experience these moments of recognition, this plot element is closely connected to Johannine characterization.

Exploring Johannine Characterization

The discussion of characters that follows is grounded in three ideas. First, a literary perspective analyzes individual figures in the Gospel as characters rather than real people. This can be difficult to grasp if one is accustomed to thinking of the Gospel as simply reporting on historical events. But remember, literary analysis of the Gospel is concerned with the narrative representation of characters and events, not with the questions of their historicity. Culpepper puts it this way: "Even if one is disposed to see real, historical persons behind every character in John and actual events in every episode, the question of how the author chose to portray the person still arises. With what techniques or devices has he made a living person live on paper, and how is this 'person' related to the rest of the narrative?"[14] To borrow another analogy, a Johannine character such as Nicodemus is not a real person any more than a painting of an apple is a real apple. Recognizing this is not to make a historical judgment on either the existence of apples or of a historical Nicodemus.[15]

Second, ancient authors thought about characters in a different way than authors of modern novels. Contemporary authors typically attempt to portray a character's psychological complexity, so that a character's development becomes the main focus of the work. But as we saw, Aristotle thought that the plot of a drama took precedence over the development of characters. The point of acting, he argued, was not to portray character, rather "the characters are for the sake of the action" (*Poetics* 6.10). This also appears to be the case with the Gospel narrative. No Johannine character shows signs of the complexity or psychological development that one finds in characters in contemporary novels. For this reason, our study of Johannine characterization should be closely linked to study of the Johannine plot.

Third, given the relationship between characters and plot, we should be cautious about assessing Johannine characters as though they were individuals with freedom of choice. Past approaches to Johannine characterization have tended to evaluate characters based on their responses to Jesus. This often takes the form of positioning individual characters on a continuum between belief and unbelief.

There are two main problems with this approach. First, it is often difficult to know where to situate individual characters on such a continuum. Is Nicodemus a believer or not? What about the Samaritan woman? Neither one of these characters offers statements of belief. Yet Nicodemus appears sympathetic toward Jesus, and the Samaritan woman facilitates the belief of her entire village. Meanwhile, other characters who do confess belief in Jesus give indications of wavering commitment. Peter claims that Jesus is "the Holy One of God" but then denies his discipleship when he is pressed. Similarly, Martha offers the most complete confession in the Gospel, but then questions Jesus's actions. She worries about the stench that will accompany the dead body of Lazarus when Jesus asks for his tomb to be opened. In short, if the author meant for readers to measure Johannine characters as particular types of belief versus unbelief, he did not make it easy to do so. Many of the characters display varying degrees of ambiguity with respect to what they know or believe about Jesus.

The second problem with this approach to Johannine characters is the fact that they are *not* real people. Real people arguably have the possibility of weighing evidence and making choices for themselves. The Gospel characters do not. In speaking of the motif of recognition in the Gospel, Jo-Ann Brant helpfully brings these two problems together:

> Modern readers have a tendency to treat recognition in the Fourth Gospel as a function of character rather than plot. Nicodemus's failure to recognize Jesus is treated as a failure of character. The logic of which characters are chosen to overcome [this lack of recognition] and which characters remain mired in it may also prove to be a function of plot. The characters who recognize Jesus have no power to prevent the plot from unfolding as it must.[16]

To this we could add that the characters who *do not* recognize Jesus also have no power to change the plot.

To be sure, there are places where Jesus directly asks characters if they believe in him (9:35; 11:26). This seems to indicate that the characters can make choices. On the other hand, Jesus also says that no one can come to him "unless drawn by the Father who sent me" (6:44). Similarly, in his prayer during the farewell meal, he reiterates that his revelation was for those who were given to him by God. He states: "I have made your name known to those whom you gave me from the world. They were yours, and you gave them to me, and they have kept your word" (17:6). Moreover, according to the narrator, Jesus "knew what was in everyone" (2:25). And finally, the narrator also flat-out claims that certain people "could not believe" because they were fulfilling scripture (12:39-40).

All of this is to reiterate that we do better to read character in relation to plot than to evaluate individual characters on the basis of belief versus unbelief. Doing so opens up the experience of reading the Gospel in a different way. Again, Brant is helpful in showing what difference it makes: "Those who look at characterization as an index of a person's character try to reconstruct thoughts and motive. Those who look at characterization as part of the coherence of action [=plot] watch as choices lead to tragic consequences, not only for Jesus, but also for those who make the choices."[17] In what follows, I will show how this "watching" of characters in relation to plot makes a difference in understanding how the Gospel works.

Recognizing the Stranger: Plot and Johannine Characterization

As discussed above, the recognition scene is a major plot element of the Gospel. It works hand in hand with the Gospel's primary focus on the identity of Jesus. Not every scene between Jesus and individual characters fits the definition of a recognition scene. Nevertheless, for those that do, the character functions as the "recognizer," such as Thomas and Mary Magdalene in chapter 20. Meanwhile, as the "recognized," Jesus is also a character in the Gospel. He is the one marked by divinity, which others may or may not recognize.

In what follows, I will focus on the characters who interact with Jesus, postponing discussion of the characters of Jesus and of God to the next chapter. Here are three examples of characters that function as recognizers like Thomas and Mary Magdalene.[18]

Nathaniel

Larsen shows how chapter 1 presents a series of four recognition scenes as the disciples begin to gather around Jesus. These scenes follow a pattern where (1) Jesus moves toward a character, (2) the character recognizes Jesus, (3) the character witnesses to another character about Jesus. The encounter between Jesus and Nathaniel in 1:45-51 is the final and most detailed in this series. Note that it is an example of a mutual recognition scene. Jesus first identifies Nathaniel as "an Israelite in whom there is no deceit." But again notice that Jesus is not *just* realizing something about Nathaniel. He already has extraordinary knowledge of Nathaniel, and this omniscience serves as a marker of Jesus's own identity. Jesus's knowledge of Nathaniel brings about Nathaniel's recognition of Jesus. In this case, Nathaniel's new knowledge results in his claim, "Rabbi, you are the Son of God! You are the King of Israel!" (1:49). This is not the end of the scene, however. Jesus issues a final statement: "Do you believe because I told you that I saw you under the fig tree? You will see greater things than these." And he said to him, "Very truly, I tell you, you will see heaven opened and the angels of God ascending and descending upon the Son of Man" (1:50-51).

There are several important aspects to note about this reply. First, although it may seem as a rebuke of Nathaniel, a closer look suggests otherwise. In the Greek text, the "you" to whom Jesus speaks is in the plural form, indicating that the point is meant for a wider audience than just Nathaniel. Second, the promise to see angels ascending and descending on the Son of Man is a clear allusion to the image of Jacob's ladder in Genesis (Gen 28:10-19). The statement suggests that rather than angels of God, it is Jesus who mediates between the cosmic and earthly realms. Thus, this closing comment by Jesus in 1:50-51 prepares the *readers* themselves to "see" and recognize the true nature of the Jesus who was introduced in the Prologue.

The Samaritan Woman

Another recognition scene occurs in chapter 4 where Jesus's dialogue partner is an unnamed woman from Samaria whom he encounters at a well at noon.[19] The exchange between Jesus and the woman intersects with many elements of recognition scenes in Greek literature. First, these scenes often involve themes of hospitality in which a stranger who enters a foreign town needs information and assistance. Such is seemingly the case in John 4, where the Johannine Jesus presents himself as a thirsty traveler. In ancient literature including the Bible, such hospitality scenes often function as an indication of a person's virtue, insofar as the host unknowingly entertains a divine guest in disguise. This is not what happens in John 4. Rather than rushing to draw water, the woman questions Jesus's request. For his part, Jesus immediately turns the conversation toward the woman's lack of knowledge (v. 10).

Unlike the scene with Nathaniel, Jesus does not immediately offer a token by which he can be recognized. Instead, he speaks enigmatically, withholding the marks of divinity and seemingly toying with the woman with his puzzling comments. Larsen suggests that this delay in revelation is a sort of test, not so much of the woman as it is of the reader. Although the woman initially fails to pass the test, the reader does. This sort of testing "confirms the reader's sense of being on a level of knowledge superior to the story actors."[20] Once again, as in the case of Nathaniel, Jesus's exchange with the character extends outward from the story-world toward the reader's progress in understanding Jesus.

When the woman fails to understand Jesus's figurative talk of living water as a reference to his life-giving presence, he once again displays his extraordinary knowledge as a recognition token: "Jesus said to her, 'Go, call your husband, and come back.' The woman answered him, 'I have no husband.' Jesus said to her, 'You are right in saying, "I have no husband"; for you have had five husbands, and the one you have now is not your husband. What you have said is true!'" (4:16-18).

Although many commentators have taken this comment as a reflection of the woman's lack of moral character, nothing in the passage supports that interpretation. Instead, Jesus's remark about the woman's intimate personal life displays the same type of omniscience that he showed to Nathaniel. It functions as a marker of Jesus's identity, not as a description of the woman's character. That this is the case is confirmed by the woman's response, "Sir, I see that you are a prophet" (v. 19). With this knowledge, she exhibits only a partial recognition of Jesus. Their conversation soon progresses so that Jesus not only shows but also *tells* the woman about his identity. When the woman expresses what she knows about the messiah, Jesus uses it as an opportunity for self-revelation: "I am he, the one who is speaking to you" (4:25-26).

Note that the pattern that was established in chapter 1 occurs here too—the one who recognizes becomes a witness, which leads to another instance of recognition. The woman runs to the village and shares what she has experienced—a man with special knowledge who is possibly the messiah! The end result of the woman's recognition is that the entire village recognizes Jesus as the "savior of the world" (4:42).

The Formerly Blind Man

A third example of the recognition scene occurs in chapter 9—the story of the man born blind. For several reasons, this is a more complex example than either the exchange with Nathaniel or the one with the Samaritan woman. First, the episode is distinctive because the Johannine Jesus is absent across much of the action. He is no longer on the scene after the healing and only returns toward the end of the story. Second, the story of the man born blind involves recognition on two levels. The crowd and then the Pharisees must recognize that the man who now sees is actually the same person as the formerly blind man. Moreover, the blind man must himself recognize the true identity of Jesus.

We see these two levels at work as the narrative progresses through a series of interrogations. First, the healed man's neighbors question him: "The neighbors and those who had seen him before as a beggar began to ask, 'Is this not the man who used to sit and beg?' Some were saying, 'It is he.' Others were saying, 'No, but it is someone like him.' He kept saying, 'I am the man'" (9:8-12).

Next the Jewish authorities interrogate the man (9:13-17), and then his parents, saying to them, "Is this your son, who you say was born blind? How then does he now see?" (9:19). Finally, they return to question the man for a second time (9:24-34).

Note that proper identification of the man is intricately related to the recognition of Jesus. The once blind, but now-seeing man functions as a token of the identity of Jesus. Proper recognition of this man as the one who was blind is a step toward proper recognition of Jesus. In this case, the Jewish authorities react with resistance, rejecting the token and its significance for the identity of Jesus. From the beginning to the end, the Pharisees claim that Jesus is "not from God." Such a claim is the exact opposite of the truth that Jesus is "from God" (9:15) within the story-world of the Gospel.

Meanwhile, the man seems to gradually gain more knowledge about Jesus and more boldness vis-à-vis Jesus's opponents. He first describes Jesus as "the man called Jesus" (9:11), then identifies him as a prophet (9:17). In his second exchange with the Jews, the man first provokes them by asking whether they "also" want to become his disciples and then challenges their position, arguing that Jesus *must* be a man from God (9:30-33). In this way, the unnamed man shows development across his brief appearance in the Gospel. This development culminates when the man again encounters Jesus. As with the Samaritan woman, Jesus offers a decisive *telling* of his identity: "Jesus heard that they had driven him out, and when he found him, he said, 'Do you believe in the Son of Man?' He answered, 'And who is he, sir? Tell me, so that I may believe in him.' Jesus said to him, 'You have seen him, and the one speaking with you is he'" (9:35-37).

At this point, the man offers a full-throated confession of faith and "worships" him. The scene ends with a final pronouncement from Jesus that points to the symbolic meaning of the healing/recognition scene:

> Jesus said, "I came into this world for judgment so that those who do not see may see, and those who do see may become blind." Some of the Pharisees near him heard this and said to him, "Surely we are not blind, are we?" Jesus said to them, "If you were blind, you would not have sin. But now that you say, 'We see,' your sin remains." (9:39-41)

In sum, the man's physical eye-opening is not the main point of the story. The central aim is to relate the man's recognition of Jesus. Meanwhile, the problem with the Pharisees is precisely their claim to "see" when they do *not* recognize who Jesus is.

Ultimately, Larsen argues that these scenes of recognition of the Johannine Jesus also involve a social integration into a certain community. As he concludes, "Whereas Jesus was a stranger to begin with, the Johannine recognitions of Jesus establish a mutual indwelling between God and his own."[21]

More Johannine Characters and More Approaches to Johannine Characterization

In spite of the pervasiveness of the theme of recognition (and one could include additional recognition scenes along with the ones discussed above), this theme does not explain *every* Johannine character. Here I look at several more examples of characters (or character groups) who present particular challenges for interpretation.

The Puzzling Case of Nicodemus

Nicodemus is one such character. As mentioned earlier, Nicodemus resists easy categorization on the basis of belief or unbelief. A brief review of his three appearances in the narrative will make clear why this is so.

In John 3, Nicodemus is introduced as a Pharisee and a leader of "the Jews." Moreover, he comes to Jesus at night. In the larger context of the

Gospel, none of this description bodes well for Nicodemus. Then, when he conveys information that would seemingly be welcome to Jesus— "Rabbi, we know that you are a teacher who has come from God; for no one can do these signs that you do apart from the presence of God" (3:2)—Jesus shifts the conversation to who is able to "see" the kingdom of God. The conversation proceeds by way of misunderstanding, with Nicodemus reduced to questions. And the scene does not end well for him. He is chastised by Jesus for his lack of comprehension as a "teacher of Israel" and then simply fades from view as Jesus's discourse continues. Given this, Culpepper suggests that John 3 is an example of a failed recognition scene. Nicodemus has not recognized who Jesus is and has failed to understand his teaching.

In light of this supposed failure, many scholars have read Nicodemus as a representative of "the Jews" in general. They argue that he comes to Jesus in darkness and remains in darkness, as Jesus's further teaching implies. Moreover, Jesus switches to the plural pronoun for "you" in the following passage, suggesting that more than just Nicodemus is in view: "Very truly, I tell you [Gk. singular], we speak of what we know and testify to what we have seen; yet you [Gk. plural] do not receive our testimony. If I have told you [Gk. plural] about earthly things and you [Gk. plural] do not believe, how can you [Gk. plural] believe if I tell you [Gk. plural] about heavenly things?" (3:11-12).

But Nicodemus appears two other times in the narrative in ways that complicate this interpretation. Some readers have supposed that these two occurrences paint a more positive picture of Nicodemus. The second time occurs in the context of a meeting of the Pharisees. Following a failed attempt by the temple police to arrest Jesus, the Pharisees challenge their seeming reluctance with the question, "Has any one of the authorities or of the Pharisees believed in him?" (7:48). Suddenly, Nicodemus reenters the narrative. Not only that, he enters the story in at least a partial defense of Jesus: "Nicodemus, who had gone to Jesus before, and who was one of them, asked, 'Our law does not judge people without first giving them a hearing to find out what they are doing, does it?'" (7:50-51).

Does the narrator emphasize that Nicodemus was "one of them" to reinforce his association with Jesus's opponents? Or, is the point to suggest that he *is* in fact one of the authorities who believed in Jesus?

This latter reading seems to be strengthened by his third and final appearance at 19:39-40. There he accompanies Joseph of Arimathea (who is described as a secret disciple for fear of "the Jews"). Nicodemus brings an extraordinary amount of spices to anoint the crucified body of Jesus for burial. Joseph is described as a "secret" disciple of Jesus. Is this a secret that is also kept from Nicodemus, or is Nicodemus by implication also a secret disciple? If the latter, what does it mean that he never confesses belief in Jesus?

Another negative interpretation sees Nicodemus functioning as a foil to the Samaritan woman who appears in the next chapter. He is named; she is not. He is Jewish; she is Samaritan. He is a man with some authority; she is a woman with none. He comes by night; she meets Jesus at noon. Nicodemus is confused and Jesus seems to chide him for this. Yet when the woman is confused, Jesus both shows and tells her who he is. As a result, she witnesses about Jesus to others.

Finally, given these conflicting details and conflicting interpretations, one can understand why some interpreters have argued that Nicodemus's primary trait is ambiguity. This has both been understood negatively, insofar as the Gospel insists on a clear choice, and positively, insofar as it may realistically represent the difficulty of consistently being an open disciple of Jesus.

There may be yet another way of understanding Nicodemus. First, according to Larsen, the initial scene with Nicodemus should *not* be viewed as a recognition scene. Jesus offers no clear token of recognition, only enigmatic speech. Consider the conversation in chapter 3 again. As we have seen, Nicodemus opens with a claim that Jesus must be from God given the signs that he does. But rather than affirming this knowledge, Jesus responds with an enigmatic statement. Only those "who are born *anōthen* can see the kingdom of God" (3:3). If you are not sure what *anōthen* means, you understand Nicodemus's position. In Greek, the term *anōthen* has two meanings. It can mean "from above" or it can mean "again." Nicodemus's incredulous question that follows suggests that he has chosen the second meaning—"How can anyone be born after having grown old? Can one enter a second time into the mother's womb and be born?" (3:4). Jesus continues with equally enigmatic language about being born of water, spirit, and wind, to which Nicodemus essentially responds with "Huh?" ("How can these things be?" [3:9]). Jesus replies with yet another question: "Are you a teacher of Israel, and yet you do not understand these things?" (3:10).

Beyond Nicodemus's initial puzzlement, there is no further indication of his reaction. He simply drops out of the story. In chapter 3, he seems to function as a foil for Jesus to offer a more extended discourse about his significance. In any case, we hear no more from Nicodemus at this point. Perhaps with the Jewish teacher Nicodemus and the Samaritan woman, the author means to contrast Jesus's "own" who did not accept him and others who do. The problem with this reading, however, is that Nicodemus is never given the same chance to recognize Jesus as is the Samaritan woman. Nicodemus starts out with quite a positive statement about the identity of Jesus and ends up with a rebuke before dropping out of the story. She begins with a challenge to Jesus but is given the means to grow in her recognition of him. If the author is attempting a contrast, it seems that it would express more the difference in how Jesus responds to these two characters than in the characters themselves.

The Beloved Disciple

As we saw in the previous chapter, historical critics of the Gospel focus on how this figure may relate to the authorship of the Gospel. Literary critics examine the role the character plays in the narrative. Most scholars conclude that he represents the "ideal" disciple and a model of discipleship for the readers. It is true that this disciple shares a special place of intimacy with Jesus. When he first enters the narrative, he is described as reclining "on [Jesus's] breast" (*en tō kolpō*) and as "the one whom Jesus loved" (13:23). The first expression is nearly identical to the one used in John 1:18 that describes Jesus as being "in the breast" of his Father (*eis ton kolpon*). Thus, the disciple's closeness to Jesus is like Jesus's closeness to his Father.

A second appearance of the disciple also suggests a place of privilege with respect to Jesus. He is present at the foot of the cross where the Johannine Jesus establishes a new relationship between the disciple and his mother (19:26). There are many theories about what this scene means. At the literal level of the narrative, it may simply be the depiction of Jesus providing for the care of his mother before his death. Symbolically, perhaps the point is to inaugurate the new family of God that begins with the death of Jesus. In either case, the disciple again stands out as one who is given a special status.

In three out of the four scenes in which he appears, the beloved disciple is paired with Peter. In the first scene, the disciple is closer to Jesus than is Peter, who must appeal to the beloved disciple to ask Jesus to identify which of his disciples will betray him (13:23-25). In chapter 20, he outruns Peter to the empty tomb. Twice the narrator mentions that the disciple reached the tomb before Peter (20:8-10). In both of these scenes, it appears the author was working with familiar traditions about Jesus and giving the beloved disciple a place in those traditions. Notice that in 13:27-28, even though Peter and the beloved disciple have just sought information from Jesus, and even though Jesus provides a clue (a recognition token!) for revealing the betrayer, the narrator goes on to say that no one at the table knew what Jesus was talking about. It is as though the exchange between Peter and the beloved disciple never took place, which would have been the situation in another version of the story that the author was adapting.

A more detailed look at the scene at the empty tomb will also show how the author shaped earlier stories to include the beloved disciple in them. This is a scene that complicates the picture of the "ideal" disciple. Here is what happens at the tomb: "Then the other disciple, who reached the tomb first, also went in, and he saw and believed; for as yet they did not understand the scripture, that he [Jesus] must rise from the dead. Then the disciples returned to their homes" (20:8-10).

On the one hand, the claim that the disciple saw and believed could be a statement of belief in Jesus. This is a common interpretation. On the other hand, this interpretation does not fit well with the statements that follow. Neither the beloved disciple nor Peter understands the scriptures "that he must rise from the dead." Then, they simply go home.

Compare this scene to the version of the empty tomb story in Luke's Gospel. In this case, women report the empty tomb to the apostles, and most of the male apostles don't believe them. But note Peter's response:

> Then they remembered his words, and returning from the tomb, they told all this to the eleven and to all the rest. Now it was Mary Magdalene, Joanna, Mary the mother of James, and the other women with them who told this to the apostles. But these words seemed to them an idle tale, and they did not believe them. But Peter got up and ran to the tomb; stooping and looking in, he saw the linen cloths by themselves; then he went home, amazed at what had happened. (Luke 24:8-12)

The parallels with the Johannine version are striking, except that in John's version, the beloved disciple runs with Peter to the tomb. And, unlike the apostles in Luke, the beloved disciple "sees" the evidence in the tomb and "believes" Mary's report.[22] Then, as in the Lukan version, both Peter and the beloved disciple go home. This is not to suggest that the Gospel writer sees the disciple in a negative light. But, the scene does not support the view that he suddenly came to "resurrection faith" as is often supposed. Instead, it shows another instance where the beloved disciple has been inserted into an earlier tradition about Peter so that he is also part of the action.

Finally, in chapter 21, Peter's question to Jesus about the beloved disciple results in a rumor that the disciple would not die (21:20-23). And, as we saw in chapter 2, this disciple is linked to witnessing and writing down "these things" (21:24).

Taken together, these scenes indicate that another important literary function of the beloved disciple is to (1) give him a place of prominence in the Gospel especially with respect to Peter, and (2) present him as responsible for transmitting the traditions about Jesus that are found in the Gospel. But we should emphasize again that the author never gives a name

71

to this character! We cannot know whether a particular historical figure was meant, or whether this is a literary device ensuring a sense of apostolic authority for these Johannine traditions that is equal to the apostolic authority of Peter.

The Function of Character Groups: The Jews, the Disciples, and the Crowd

In several places in the Gospel, Jesus interacts with character groups rather than individual characters—"the Jews," the crowd, and the disciples. These character groups pose questions, misunderstand, and deliberate about the identity of Jesus. As Jo-Ann Brant has shown, in doing so, these character groups in John fulfill the functions of the collective chorus in Greek tragedies. They function as the "corporate voice of deliberation" (to use Brant's term) in the Gospel. From this perspective, "the Jews," just like "the crowd," do not represent an actual historical group who opposed Jesus, any more than the chorus of Greek tragedy represented an actual historical group. Rather, "the Jews" function in the Gospel as a constructed, theatrical identity representing a collective wider community.

This wider collective entity—whether the Jews or the Greek chorus—gives voice to the inherited traditions and wisdom of the culture in which the narrative is embedded. In Greek drama the collective voice of the chorus is a way of contextualizing the tragedy in traditional Greek culture. In the tragedies, the chorus offers conventional wisdom, often in a way that shows the limitations of that same wisdom. Likewise, in the Gospel of John, the Jews and sometimes the crowd interpret Jesus's actions by way of traditional claims of Judaism. Their collective speech also demonstrates the limitations of those traditional claims for understanding Jesus.

The following passages show how the crowd functions in this way. In the context of a Jewish festival in Jerusalem, the crowd debates and deliberates about the messianic identity of Jesus.

> And there was considerable complaining about him among the crowds. While some were saying, "He is a good man," others were saying, "No, he is deceiving the crowd." (7:12)

When they heard these words, some in the crowd said, "This is really the prophet." Others said, "This is the Messiah." But some asked, "Surely the Messiah does not come from Galilee, does he? Has not the scripture said that the Messiah is descended from David and comes from Bethlehem, the village where David lived?" So there was a division in the crowd because of him. (7:40-43)

Note that the verb used for "complaining" in the first passage is the same verb used about the Israelites who complained in the wilderness about Moses. This verb also appears in chapter 6 with reference to both the Jews and the disciples complaining, or murmuring, about Jesus (6:41, 43, 63).

The same deliberation is evident in the following passages. In these examples, the collective voice comes from the Jews, as they respond to claims that Jesus has made. Note that in the first passage, the narrator has already indicated that many of the Jews believed in Jesus (8:30). But Jesus continues to press them, leading them to make their own claims about their tradition. In the second example, we again see the Jews divided and deliberating about how to understand Jesus.

Then Jesus said to the Jews who had believed in him, "If you continue in my word, you are truly my disciples; and you will know the truth, and the truth will make you free." They answered him, "We are descendants of Abraham and have never been slaves to anyone. What do you mean by saying, 'You will be made free'?" (8:31-33)

Again the Jews were divided because of these words. Many of them were saying, "He has a demon and is out of his mind. Why listen to him?" Others were saying, "These are not the words of one who has a demon. Can a demon open the eyes of the blind?" (10:19-21)

Many literary critical readings assume that the Jews simply represent unbelief in the Gospel. This interpretation corresponds to the broader notion that the characters represent particular responses to Jesus, thereby confronting the reader with making their own choice of belief versus unbelief. But Brant suggests something different: "The deliberation of the various groups of Jews is not a device that invites the audience to choose one of two positions; instead, it is an opportunity for the audience to observe the inner workings of the mind of the other, whose perspective it does not share and who makes clear that recognizing Jesus is no easy matter."[23]

As mentioned, at times even the disciples assume a collective deliberative role. Like "the Jews," the disciples have occasions of misunderstanding and questioning. Moreover, the disciples are not immune to the division that occurs in the crowd and "the Jews." When Jesus speaks of the necessity of "eating and drinking his flesh," some complain just like the crowd and the Jews (6:60-61). And soon, the narrator reports that "many of his disciples turned back" and "no longer went about with him" (6:66).

At other places, the disciples also act as disciples of a teacher should act—they are alongside Jesus at many points of his ministry (e.g., 1:39; 6:3; 11:16; 18:1), looking after his material needs and following his instructions (4:8, 31; 6:8-13). Another important function of the disciples is that they remember what Jesus said after his death and resurrection as well as what scripture said in relation to Jesus (2:22, 27; 12:16). This function is particularly important for the reader because it reinforces the truth of Jesus's promise to his disciples during the farewell meal. "But the Advocate [Gk. *paraklētos*], the Holy Spirit, whom the Father will send in my name, will teach you everything, and remind you of all that I have said to you" (14:26). When the narrative points forward to this future remembering of the disciples, it demonstrates the fulfillment of this promise and the active role of the *paraklētos*. I discuss this figure more fully in the next chapter.

Overall, mixed portrayals of these character groups suggest they do not play only one role in the Gospel. The narrator uses them as a literary device to different effect and different points in the story.

More on Greek Drama and the Gospel: What Difference Does It Make?

We have seen how literary interpretation of the "world in the text" produces different results than if we focus on historical reconstruction of the "world behind the text." This last section of the chapter will highlight some additional instances where recognition of dramatic conventions produces alternative explanations for what we see in the Gospel.

Scholars have noticed the way the Gospel writer seemingly "staged" the encounters between characters in the narrative. Greek dramas typically feature only two characters (or character groups) on stage at the same time. This is also the case in the Gospel. The trial before Pilate in chapters 18–19 demonstrates this most clearly. Here Pilate moves inside and outside of his headquarters, alternating between confrontations with Jesus and with the Jews. In chapter 9, the series of interrogations between the Pharisees, the man born blind, and his parents follows a similar pattern where only two groups interact at a time. This type of parallel with dramatic conventions in the ancient world has encouraged scholars to do even more careful comparison between the Gospel and elements of Greek drama.

This comparative work has led to new hypotheses about the composition of the Gospel that differ from those proposed by historical critics. For instance, recall that when historical critics observed a break in the narrative between chapters 14 and 15, they suggested that the material in chapters 15–17 was added to the Gospel later. But evidence from Greek tragedies suggests another possibility. George Parsenios shows that the Gospel writer may have fashioned the farewell meal of Jesus on the model of other Greek scenes of departure toward death. Significantly, he shows that the type of break that is evident between chapters 14 and 15 is also present in departure to death speeches in Greek drama. According to Parsenios, in such scenes the delay in departure allows the character to go on speaking, much like the Johannine Jesus does in chapters 15–17.[24] Therefore, this narrative interruption alone is not a sufficient reason to think that chapters 15–17 were added, since they can now be explained as a literary convention.

Similarly, Brant argues that the Gospel's depiction of Jesus and the Jews in heated exchange can look different if one is familiar with the conventions of Greek tragedy. Tragedies often feature exchanges of insults between characters. The point is to best one's opponents through a show of wits and provocation. In the Greek tragic genre, these battles of wits are not meant to vilify a particular character, but to score points with the audience. The Gospel shares in this generic convention of verbal conflict by showing Jesus hurling insults at his opponents. The Gospel also follows the tragic convention by characterizing Jesus's opposition as hostile or ignorant. But even this should not necessitate the vilification of one side of the contest by the audience. Indeed, for centuries the misreading of a dramatic opposition between characters (the Johannine Jesus vs. "the Jews") as an ontological truth about the nature of the Jewish people has produced one historical tragedy after another. As Brant notes, when one pulls the Gospel's dramatic polemic into a world where there are individuals who are Jews rather than Christians, it leads to the legacy of "blood libel, pogrom, ghetto, and *Shoah*."[25]

Other Literary Devices in the Gospel of John

In what follows I outline some of the other literary devices that contribute to the Johannine narrative. Many of these are ways of using language that are also common to Greek drama—especially the use of irony. Although I discuss them below under separate headings, all of these devices are intricately interwoven—riddles, double meanings, and irony work hand in hand, while symbolic and metaphorical language are interwoven throughout the narrative. Culpepper helpfully describes these types of literary elements as part of the "implicit commentary" of the Gospel. As he puts it, "In John, the reader finds that the evangelist says a great deal without actually saying it. Having drawn readers to his side by means of the Prologue, the evangelist trusts them to pick up on the overtones of his language."[26] Such implicit communication is yet another way that the Gospel writer manages to build a story-world, while simultaneously building a bridge to the Gospel audience.

Irony and Misunderstanding as Literary Elements in the Gospel

In the theatre or in a piece of literature, irony is present when the audience has more knowledge than the characters in the story-world. Irony was frequently used to great effect in Greek tragedies. Perhaps the most famous example of Greek dramatic irony is Sophocles's *Oedipus Rex*. When the audience listens to Oedipus vow to hunt down King Laius's killer, they know what he does not know—that Oedipus himself is the murderer. In the Gospel, the audience is regularly given special insight that is unavailable to most of the characters in the narrative. For example, the Prologue makes clear that Jesus is the light that has come into the world, and Jesus himself declares that he is the light of the world (1:9; 8:12; 9:5). Thus, the audience can perceive the irony later in the narrative when Jesus's opponents come with "lanterns and torches" to arrest him (18:3). A similar form of irony occurs when Jesus, who has earlier declared that he is the way, the truth, and the life (14:6), is later asked by Pilate, "What is truth?" (18:38).

Aside from Jesus, the characters themselves are unaware of the nuances of ironic language, even when they are speaking ironically themselves. And, at times, the narrator steps into the story to be sure the audience "gets it." This means providing special knowledge that highlights the irony. Not only does this make the story more interesting for the audience, it also creates a feeling of inclusion. They become part of an inner circle that has the insight and knowledge to understand the truths of the Gospel.

Consider, for example, the irony expressed through the high priest Caiaphas. Following Jesus's raising of Lazarus, the Jewish council worries that he will attract even more followers, so that "the Romans will come and destroy both our holy place and our nation" (11:48). Caiaphas responds, "You know nothing at all! You do not understand that it is better for you to have one man die for the people than to have the whole nation destroyed." At this point, the narrator provides an explanation: "He did not say this on his own, but being high priest that year he prophesied that Jesus was about to die for the nation, and not for the nation only, but to gather into one the dispersed children of God" (11:49-52).

There is irony upon irony here. The Jewish high priest Caiaphas arrogantly declares that his colleagues know nothing. But from the audience's perspective their prediction about the Roman destruction of Judea in 70 CE (before the Gospel was written) is all too accurate. In addition, the author once again uses a word with multiple meanings to introduce deeper irony. In this case, it concerns the use of the Greek word *hyper*. It can mean many things, including "for," "instead of," and "on behalf of." The NRSV translates the word as "for" both in Caiaphas's statement, "for the people" and in the narrator's explanation, "for the nation."

...better for you to have one man die *for the people* (11:50, emphasis added)

...he prophesied that Jesus was about to die *for the nation* (11:51, emphasis added)

In the Greek, the italicized phrase is exactly the same: "*hyper tou ethnos.*" But in the first statement *hyper* is better translated "instead of" the people. The high priest means to put him to death to prevent the deaths of others.

The second statement should be translated "on behalf of" pointing to the vicarious nature of Jesus's death (a point to which we return in the next chapter). In this way, the author constructs a scene in which the Jewish high priest, who is steadfastly opposed to Jesus, unwittingly articulates the saving significance of Jesus's death.

In some cases, a reader who does not understand irony in the narrative will completely miss the point. In John 7, a crowd, this time described as people from Jerusalem, deliberates about whether Jesus is the messiah: "Now some of the people of Jerusalem were saying, 'Is not this the man whom they are trying to kill? And here he is, speaking openly, but they say nothing to him! Can it be that the authorities really know that this is the Messiah? Yet we know where this man is from; but when the Messiah comes, no one will know where he is from'" (7:25-27). Then Jesus cries out while teaching in the temple, "You know me, and you know where I am from" (7:28). Taken at face value, Jesus's words sound like an affirmation of the people's claim to know Jesus's origins. It is decidedly not. Rather, his statement is ironic, as if he had said: "So you think you know me and where I'm from?!" He is raising the issue of truly knowing him, which has nothing to do with knowing his hometown of Nazareth (which the author does not mention here, but see 1:45; 18:5; 19:19). This is clear from Jesus's own assertion that they do not know who sent him (God), nor that he comes from God. Unless one reads Jesus's initial statement ironically, indeed as sarcasm, this whole passage will not make sense.

One final example of extended irony occurs in Jesus's trial before Pilate (18:28–19:16). In the passion narrative, Jesus is mocked, dressed in purple robes, and crowned with a crown of thorns. This "mock coronation" is a traditional part of the passion narrative, but in the Gospel of John, there is a heightened sense of irony created by shaping the scene so that Jesus appears before the crowd of Jews, dressed in royal attire. The scene follows on a discussion between Pilate and Jesus about kingship, and is followed by Pilate's insistence that Jesus is king of the Jews. At the story level, Pilate is orchestrating events seemingly to mock both Jesus and the Jews with references to Jesus's supposed "kingship." Yet on the level of an audience who knows that Jesus is the messiah, the dressing of Jesus in royal attire and labeling him as "king of the Jews" represents a proper understanding of his significance.

Irony works hand in hand with the use of double meanings, and misunderstanding is a regular part of Jesus's encounter with other characters in the narrative. One way the author creates these moments of confusion is by using words that have more than one meaning. Unfortunately, these nuances are often lost in translation. One can only understand Nicodemus's confusion if one knows that the Greek word *anōthen* has two meanings—"again" and "from above."

Consider their exchange as translated in the NRSV. "Jesus answered him, 'Very truly, I tell you, no one can see the kingdom of God without being born from above.' Nicodemus said to him, 'How can anyone be born after having grown old? Can one enter a second time into the mother's womb and be born?'" (3:3-4).

Nicodemus's question about being born a second time after growing old only makes sense if he has taken *anōthen* to mean "again." But because the English translation has Jesus saying born "from above," the textual play on the double meaning of the word is not apparent.

In John 4, a similar wordplay involves a discussion of "living water" (Gk. *hydōr zōn*). When Jesus tells the Samaritan woman that he can supply her with "living water," she reasonably thinks he means flowing water rather than well water. She hears in his comment an extraordinary claim that will keep her from having to make daily trips to lug water from the well. But Jesus is speaking again in a figurative way. "Living water" refers not to literal flowing water but to the spiritual nourishment that he offers.

In other places Jesus seems to speak in riddles. He does this with many different characters. Here are two examples. Notice how the riddle that is voiced by Jesus results in confused questions from his listeners.

To the Jews:

> Again he said to them, "I am going away, and you will search for me, but you will die in your sin. Where I am going, you cannot come." Then the Jews said, "Is he going to kill himself? Is that what he means by saying, 'Where I am going, you cannot come'?" (8:21-22)

To the disciples:

> "A little while, and you will no longer see me, and again a little while, and you will see me." Then some of his disciples said to one another, "What does he mean by saying to us, 'A little while, and you will no longer see me, and again a little while, and you will see me'; and 'Because I am going to the Father'?" They said, "What does he mean by this 'a little while'? We do not know what he is talking about." (16:16-18)

Later, during the farewell meal with the disciples, the Johannine Jesus acknowledges his enigmatic way of speaking by suggesting that he can speak otherwise.

> "I have said these things to you in figures of speech. The hour is coming when I will no longer speak to you in figures, but will tell you plainly of the Father." (16:25; see also 10:24; 11:14)

That the "hour" for this plain speech has in fact arrived at this point in the narrative is soon confirmed by the disciples' reply: "Yes, now you are speaking plainly, not in any figure of speech!" (16:29). Why Jesus speaks in riddles even to his disciples is not explained. It seems simply another way that Jesus is shown to be an enigmatic figure from above who only some can recognize.

The Use of Symbolism in the Gospel

Finally, another distinctive literary element in the Gospel is its use of symbolic language. In fact, symbolism permeates the narrative from beginning to end, with certain core symbols evoked in multiple ways.

In a sense, the Johannine Jesus is the fundamental symbol in the Gospel insofar as he is a symbol for God. Beyond that, the key symbols of the Gospel are used to say more about who Jesus is and how he relates to the community of believers.

Because this language is primarily related to the significance of Jesus, we explore it more fully in the next chapter.

Chapter 4

Exploring the Theology of the Gospel of John

With this chapter, we turn from historical and literary analyses of the Gospel to a discussion of theological topics. Theology refers to the study of God as well as the study of subtopics related to belief in God. Thus, a theological approach to the Gospel typically includes analyses of what ideas the Gospel conveys about God, as well as the intricately related questions of what the Gospel communicates about Jesus (Christology), salvation (soteriology), the church (ecclesiology), and how to live a moral life in the world (ethics). This chapter will introduce you to all of these topics in relation to the Gospel.

One might expect a theological approach to the Gospel to begin with a discussion of God. But the Gospel begins with an assertion about the intimate relation between the *logos* and God (1:1). The narrator then points out that no one has seen God and that only the Son makes him known (1:19). Later, the Johannine Jesus states that no one comes to the Father except through the Son (14:6), that by seeing the Son, one sees the Father (14:9), and that by knowing the Son one knows the Father (16:7). In other words, a central claim of the Gospel is that only by knowing the Johannine Jesus can one gain a knowledge of the Johannine God. For this reason, I will begin this theological study of the Gospel with an examination of its Christology.

Here we should recall our earlier discussion about the "divinity" of the Johannine Jesus. As we will see, the author of the Gospel speaks of Jesus in a number of different ways, but he is not aware of or assuming the development of church doctrines about the relationship between Jesus and God.[1] Therefore, it would be anachronistic for us to interpret the Gospel as though later christological debates and their outcomes had already occurred. Insofar as the author considers Jesus to be "divine," it is by way of the categories that he does use. These are the categories we will explore below.

Christology in the Gospel of John

Who Is Jesus and What Does He Do?

Carefully read the verses listed below. What do you learn from these passages about who Jesus is and what he does? What questions do these statements raise for you?

On Jesus's origins: 3:31; 8:23, 42; 13:3
On Jesus's relationship with God: 5:19, 30; 10:30; 14:28
On Jesus's purpose and work in the world: 5:30; 8:15-16; 12:47

If you had some difficulty understanding how all of these claims hold together, you are not alone. Johannine scholars have long noticed that the Gospel of John offers its reader riddles about the Johannine Jesus. As we have seen, the Prologue opens with a paradoxical statement: the Word was *with* God and the Word *was* God (1:2). Such paradoxes continue through the Gospel. Jesus consistently claims that he comes from above and was sent by the Father. He also claims that he can do nothing apart from the Father, the Father is greater than him, but also that he and the Father are one. Jesus moves between claims that he judges (5:30), that he was given authority to judge (5:27), and also that he does not judge (8:15; 12:47). I highlight them here to demonstrate that studying Johannine Christology is no easy task. Scholarly attempts to resolve tensions such as these are wide-ranging to say the least.[2] The discussion of Johannine Christology in this chapter will focus on four questions: (1) What does the Gospel communicate about the divine and/or human status of Jesus? (2) What are the central symbols and motifs in the Gospel that contribute to understanding the Johannine Jesus? (3) What is the nature of salvation in John? and (4) What is the significance of Jesus's death?

The Humanity and the Divinity of the Johannine Jesus

"The Word became flesh and lived among us, and we have seen his glory" (John 1:14). With these words, this famous verse in the Prologue expresses what has come to be called the "incarnational" Christology of the Gospel of John. In general terms, the word *incarnation* refers to a deity taking on human form. The question for readers of the Gospel is what this bodily transformation means with respect to the status of the divine *logos*. Does God actually become human, or does the divine simply appear in human form? In the ancient world, the latter concept was a common motif in Greek dramas and novels.[3] Even in the Hebrew Bible, there are narratives that suggest a temporary incarnation of a divine being (e.g., Gen 18:1-16; 32:24-30). Far less common in these ancient writings are indications that these fleshly manifestations mean that a divine being *actually* becomes a human being. Again, although this idea will eventually become a central doctrine of the Christian church, it would not have been a self-evident interpretation of the Gospel when it was written.

A now classic scholarly debate about this topic began in the mid-twentieth century between Rudolf Bultmann and his student Ernst Käsemann. Bultmann argued that the most significant aspect of Johannine Christology is found in the first statement of John 1:14, "And the Word became flesh and lived among us." For Bultmann, it is only in the "sheer humanity" of the Johannine Jesus that he is the Revealer. The Gospel presents the reader with this paradox: "the δοχα [*doxa*, glory] is not to be seen alongside the σαρχ [*sarx*, flesh] nor through the σαρχ as through a window; it is to be seen in the σαρχ [*sarx*, flesh] and nowhere else."[4] Bultmann refers to this incarnational claim—the Word became flesh—as the "offense" of the Gospel. By this he means that human beings naturally expect that divine revelation will have to "prove itself." Revelation should be easily recognizable as revelation. But the Gospel, Bultmann argues, offers divine revelation as "a peculiar *hiddenness*." The offense of the Gospel is that "the Revealer is nothing but a man" and he is taken for a man by all who meet him."[5] The glory of the Johannine Jesus, according to Bultmann, can only be seen in the humanity of Jesus, not in spite of his humanity.

Käsemann argued exactly the opposite about the Gospel's Christology. In his view, the emphasis of John 1:14 is not on the reference to the flesh at the beginning of the verse, but rather in its concluding claim, "and we beheld his glory." Although the Johannine Jesus takes on human form, Käsemann insists that nothing about his presentation in the Gospel suggests that Jesus is mere man. He asks:

> In what sense is he flesh, who walks on the water and through closed doors, who cannot be captured by his enemies, who at the well of Samaria is tired and desires a drink, yet has no need of drink and has food different from that which his disciples seek? ... Not merely from the prologue and from the mouth of Thomas, but from the whole gospel [one who has eyes to see and ears to hear] can perceive the confession, "my Lord and my God."[6]

In short, Käsemann claims that the Gospel offers no realistic incarnation but rather (to use his famous formulation) a "picture of Jesus as God walking on the face of the earth."[7] While he grants that the narrative depicts some features of "lowliness," he suggests that these details are only what is minimally required for Jesus to pass as a human among humans for his time on earth. Käsemann concludes that the Gospel's presentation of Jesus is actually a "naïve docetism" and that the church mistakenly accepted the Gospel as orthodox. Käsemann leaves open the question of whether the canonization of the Gospel was a fortuitous error on the part of the church, while also pointing to the dangers of John's docetic leanings.

Docetism

The word *Docetism* comes from the Greek verb *dokein*, meaning "to seem." It is used to refer to the idea that Jesus only seemed to have a real body, and only appeared to be human. Some early strands of Christianity developed this idea, claiming that the divine Jesus never actually suffered and died on the cross. Such versions of Christianity were eventually rejected by the larger church.

This mid-twentieth-century debate about the Johannine Jesus's humanity versus divinity has continued with some scholars agreeing with Käsemann's interpretation and others mounting arguments against it.[8] For example, Meeks's analysis of the Johannine Jesus as the stranger from heaven who visits earth for a time is in keeping with Käsemann's view.[9] So, too, Jerome Neyrey sees the Johannine Jesus as one who looks back fondly at the time when he was in the presence of the Father (17:5) and eagerly anticipates resuming that position (13:1-3).[10] These interpretations emphasize the spatial and temporal aspects of the Gospel—Jesus descends to earth "from above" for only a time before ascending again to the Father.

Other interpreters of the Gospel argue against Käsemann's view.[11] Sometimes this argument comes in the form of insisting on the humanity of the Johannine Jesus by pointing to places in the Gospel where he shows basic human needs. So, for example, references to Jesus's fatigue (4:6), thirst (19:28), or displays of emotion (11:33, 35) are taken as proofs of his humanity. But lifting up such qualities as evidence of a godlike figure's humanity does not make a compelling case. In the ancient world gods were routinely depicted in anthropomorphic ways—eating, sleeping, having sex, arguing, and so on.[12] This is true both in Greek and Roman writings, as well as in the Hebrew scriptures, where God gets angry, enjoys the smell of sacrificial food offerings (e.g., Gen 8:21; Lev 1:9; 23:18), and at times seems to appear in human form enjoying an evening breeze, a hospitable meal, or a wrestling match (Gen 3:8; 18:1-16; 32:22-32). In other words, ancient gods often act like humans.

Another explanation for the Johannine picture of the divine Jesus is that the Gospel writer assumes that his readers know that Jesus was human, but are not necessarily convinced that he is divine. For this reason, the author emphasizes the divinity of Jesus throughout the Gospel, but is not concerned to prove his humanity. In this view, the Gospel's somewhat one-sided emphasis on Jesus's divinity is meant to reassure the Gospel audience about their confessed belief in Jesus (or possibly bring readers to faith; see note 1, for chapter 2, page 157).

Finally, many historical critics look for evidence from the Johannine letters to add to this debate. A statement in 1 John 4:2-3 is often read as a clue to the Johannine community's insistence on the humanity of Jesus against a group who denied it: "By this you know the Spirit of God: every spirit that confesses that Jesus Christ has come in the flesh is from God, and every spirit that does not confess Jesus is not from God."

This way of understanding the passage depends on emphasizing the phrase "in the flesh" in this verse, an emphasis that was not necessarily intended by the author. Seeing the statement as reflecting a dispute about the humanity of Jesus is one way to interpret this verse, but not the only way. One can also interpret the verse as reflecting a debate about whether Jesus was from God. We will return to this in the discussion of the Johannine epistles in chapter 6.

In the end, evidence from the Johannine writings alone does not provide a definitive answer to this twentieth-century debate about the flesh/glory of Jesus. It may well be that this particular problem—flesh versus glory—was not a concern for the author, at least as the issue has been formulated by contemporary scholars. This does not mean that exploring the theological implications of the flesh-and-glory language in the Gospel cannot be done fruitfully. Whatever the Gospel writer may have thought about Jesus, contemporary Christians now regard the confession of Jesus as fully human and fully divine as a central part of their tradition.[13] However, if we are reading the Gospel with a historical and/ or literary orientation, we should remain open to its potential strangeness, to the possibility that this ancient work may not always match our expectations.

Christological Symbols and Motifs in Johannine Literature

Even if we can't settle the humanity/divinity debate about the Johannine Jesus, we can still learn a lot about the Gospel's Christology by focusing on recurring symbols and motifs in the narrative. As we will see, these symbols are firmly rooted in the Hellenistic Jewish and Roman context in which the Gospel was written. Moreover, the Gospel links the Johannine Jesus with symbols that were central to Judaism. Certainly, this includes the royal and messianic traditions of Judaism. But the Gospel writer also makes a point of linking Jesus with the Jewish sacrificial practice centered in the Jerusalem temple, with ancestral figures like Moses, Abraham, and Jacob, and with the figure of God's wisdom.

Especially striking is the fact that these multiple associations are made already in the first chapter of the Gospel. The Prologue uses language that evokes the wisdom tradition of Israel, which I explain further below. Then in 1:19-51, one character after another calls Jesus by a title: lamb of God (v. 29), rabbi (v. 38), messiah (v. 41), Son of God (v. 49), and king of Israel (v. 49). The author apparently assumes that his audience will understand the significance of these designations. Some of them are well known from Jewish traditions (lamb of God, messiah, rabbi, king of Israel), while one would resonate more with the Gospel's Roman imperial setting (Son of God). Neither Jesus nor the narrator disputes any of these references, though Jesus seems to add one to the list, referring to himself as the Son of Man (v. 51).

Chosen One or Son of God?
A Text-Critical Question

There is yet one other title for Jesus given by John in 1:34, but we must deal with a text-critical problem in order to see it. Here are two English translations of what John announces:

"I have seen and I testify that this is God's Chosen One" (NIV).

"And I myself have seen and have testified that this is the Son of God" (NRSV).

The reason for the different titles in these English translations is that ancient Greek copies of the Gospel have different wordings for this verse. As mentioned in chapter 1, the task of a textual critic is to analyze the surviving ancient manuscripts in order to determine the original wording of a particular text.[14] This work includes considering what types of changes a scribe would be more likely to make. In this case, although there are slightly more manuscripts supporting the "Son of God" wording in 1:34, the argument for the original text reading "the chosen one of God" is more compelling. That is because it is easy to understand why a scribe would make an editorial change from the less familiar title "chosen one of God" to the far more familiar "Son of God," especially given the many other references to Jesus as "Son" in the Gospel. Or, to state the argument in reverse, it is harder to understand why a scribe would edit out the title "Son of God," in order to introduce an otherwise unfamiliar title for Jesus. Thus, we can add "chosen one of God" to the list of titles already attributed to Jesus in chapter 1. This means that in the first chapter we find four titles that relate to the notion of divinely chosen kingship in the traditions of Israel—chosen one of God, messiah, king of Israel, and son of God.

The association between Jesus and the scriptural traditions of Israel is evident in John's reference to Jesus as the "Lamb of God who takes away the sin of the world" (1:29). The phrase evokes several different traditions from ancient Israel. The most obvious is the tradition of the Passover lamb used for the Passover meal. In the Exodus story, lamb's blood is smeared on doorposts to distinguish the Hebrews from the Egyptians during God's final plague against Pharaoh (Exod 12:1-14). In this ritual practice of the Passover meal, the lamb is not used as a sacrifice to God, but rather recalls God's saving act of liberation for the Hebrews enslaved in Egypt. The animal that was traditionally sacrificed for removal of sin was not a lamb, but a goat (see Lev 16:21-22). With this, and other sin offerings described in the Torah, God provides the sacrificial means for atonement for sin.

But the Gospel writer may have in mind another scriptural tradition with the phrase. Isaiah 53, known as one of the "suffering servant" songs, describes a figure whose life will be made an offering for sin and "shall bear their iniquities" (Isa 53:10-11). This figure is also described as "a lamb that is led to the slaughter." The suffering servant figure was frequently connected to Jesus in the early Christian tradition (cf. Matt 8:17;

Acts 8:30-35). It is possible that the author saw Jesus as such a suffering servant, a "lamb of God" led to slaughter, even if he does not emphasize Jesus's suffering.

The enthusiastic application of this wide range of titles to Jesus in chapter 1 shows how deeply the Gospel is linked to the ancient traditions of Israel. The use of these titles foreshadows the way the rest of the narrative will portray Jesus as one who fulfills or surpasses the expectations of God's saving power in Jewish tradition. Indeed, the chapter ends with a promise from Jesus that "you will see greater things than these" (1:51).

Along with the Gospel's distinctive flurry of titles to usher in the early ministry of Jesus, there is another christological element that is unique to the Gospel. This is the way the Johannine Jesus frequently uses his own metaphorical language to define himself. In contrast to the commands to secrecy in the Gospel of Mark (Mark 8:30; 9:9), the Johannine Jesus speaks openly about his identity throughout the narrative. As we saw in the last chapter, he uses the Greek phrase *ego eimi* ("I am") as self-revelatory divine speech indicating his messianic identity. But, the Johannine Jesus uses the same phrase to define himself symbolically as the bread of life (6:35, 48), the living bread that comes down from heaven (6:51), the light of the world (8:12), the gate (10:7), the good shepherd (10:11), the resurrection and the life (11:25), the way, the truth, and life (14:6), and the true vine (15:1). Such self-descriptive statements are unique to the Gospel of John and offer a rich array of images alongside the traditional titles that are applied to Jesus in the Synoptic Gospels. Some of these statements evoke the life-giving significance of Jesus through basic images of sustenance such as bread, light, and life. Others share in the christological motifs we will discuss below. Light is commonly connected with God's wisdom. The shepherd imagery links with notions of the role of the protective king. And as we have seen, when these statements stand alone as simply "I am" they serve as words of theophany, indicating Jesus's divine identity (4:26; 18:6). With this, we turn to explore more fully some of the Gospel's core christological metaphors.

The Johannine Jesus as Incarnate Wisdom

As we have already seen, the Gospel opens with a poetic introduction of the *logos* and a paradox concerning the relationship between the *logos* and God: somehow this *logos*/Word is both distinct from and the same as God. Understanding the various uses of *logos* in the ancient world provides more context for considering this paradox. Although *logos* is translated simply as "word" in English, the Greek term was rich in meaning in the first century CE. In Greco-Roman philosophy, *logos* referred to the idea of a divine plan for the universe, or the rational principle that undergirded the ordered cosmos. While this was not likely its primary meaning for the Gospel writer, it does contribute to the cosmic, preexistent dimension evoked at the beginning of the Gospel. We learn more from the use of *logos* in the writings of Philo, a Hellenistic Jewish philosopher writing in the period contemporaneous to the Gospel. Philo uses *logos* frequently, sometimes to refer to divine mediators and sometimes as a way of speaking about God's wisdom. In Jewish traditions, God's wisdom (*hokma* in Hebrew, *sophia* in Greek) was understood as God's distinctive creative aspect. As Sharon Ringe notes, "wisdom is connected to the divine logic undergirding the creation—God's will or plan and the deep structures and relationships that give the world meaning, shape and coherence."[15] In the Fourth Gospel too, the *logos* is associated with God's creative power and plan for the cosmos. Apart from it, "not one thing came into being" (1:3). And this same incarnate *logos* will mediate knowledge of God to the world (1:18). Given what follows in the rest of the Gospel, it seems likely that the author used *logos* as a way of associating the Johannine Jesus with the figure of God's Wisdom.

In Jewish scriptural traditions, God's Wisdom was often expressed in personified form, taking on a female voice. The chart below highlights some of the parallels between the speeches by and about Wisdom (on the left) and the presentation of the Johannine Jesus (on the right). The bolded portions highlight parallel concepts.

Ages ago I was set up, at the first, **before the beginning of the earth....then I was beside him, like a master worker**; and I was daily his delight, rejoicing before him always. (Proverbs 8:23, 30)	**In the beginning was the Word**, and the Word was with God, and the Word was God. **He was in the beginning with God.** All things came into being through him, and without him not one thing came into being. (John 1:1-3)
"Then the Creator of all things gave me a command, and my Creator chose the place for my tent. He said, '**Make your dwelling [kataskēnōson, "pitch a tent"] in Jacob, and in Israel receive your inheritance.**'" (Sir 24:8)	**And the Word became flesh, and dwelt [eskēnōsen, "pitched a tent"] among us,** and we beheld His glory, glory as of the only begotten from the Father, full of grace and truth. (John 1:14 NASB)
"Come to me, you who desire me, and eat your fill of my fruits. For the memory of me is sweeter than honey, and the possession of me sweeter than the honeycomb. **Those who eat of me will hunger for more, and those who drink of me will thirst for more.** Whoever obeys me will not be put to shame, and those who work with me will not sin." (Sir 24:19-22)	Jesus said to her, **"Everyone who drinks of this water will be thirsty again, but those who drink of the water that I will give them will never be thirsty.** The water that I will give will become in them a spring of water gushing up to eternal life." (John 4:13-14) Those **who eat my flesh and drink my blood have eternal life,** and I will raise them up on the last day; **for my flesh is true food and my blood is true drink.** Those who eat my flesh and drink my blood abide in me, and I in them. (John 6:54-56)

My child, if you accept my words and treasure up my command- ments within you...then you will understand the fear of the LORD and find the knowledge of God. (Prov 2:1, 5)	**If you keep my commandments, you will abide in my love,** just as I have kept my Father's command- ments and abide in his love. (John 15:10)
I learned without guile and I im- part without grudging; I do not hide her wealth, for it is an un- failing treasure for mortals; **those who get it obtain friendship with God,** commended for the gifts that come from instruction. (Wis 7:13-14)	No one has greater love than this, to lay down one's life for one's **friends. You are my friends if you do what I command you.** I do not call you servants any longer, because the ser- vant does not know what the mas- ter is doing; but **I have called you friends,** because I have made known to you everything that I have heard from my Father. (John 15:13-15)
Wisdom found no place where she might dwell; Then a dwelling- place was assigned her in the heav- ens. **Wisdom went forth to make her dwelling among the children of men, And found no dwelling- place:** Wisdom returned to her place, And took her seat among the angels. (1 Enoch 42:1-2)	**He came to what was his own, and his own people did not accept him.** (John 1:11)

Because I have called and you refused, have stretched out my hand and no one heeded.... Then they will call upon me, but I will not answer; they will seek me diligently, but will not find me. (Prov 1:24, 28) You have forsaken the fountain of wisdom. If you had walked in the way of God, you would be living in peace forever. (Bar 3:12-13)	Jesus answered, "I have told you, and you do not believe. The works that I do in my Father's name testify to me; but you do not believe, because you do not belong to my sheep. (John 10:25-26) Again he said to them, "I am going away, and you will search for me, but you will die in your sin. Where I am going, you cannot come." (John 8:21)

These are just some examples of how the evangelist draws heavily on wisdom imagery in his presentation of Jesus. Notably, the Johannine Jesus regularly makes claims that *surpass* those of personified Wisdom. For example, whereas Wisdom is a budding vine producing fruit (Sir 24:17), Jesus is the "true" vine bearing branches (15:1-3). Similarly, Wisdom calls her followers to come to her and eat and drink, claiming, "Those who eat of me will hunger for more, and those who drink of me will thirst for more" (Sir 24:21). The Johannine Jesus also speaks of eating and drinking (6:53-56), but his body is "true food," and his blood is "true drink." Moreover according to the Johannine Jesus, "Whoever comes to me will never be hungry, and whoever believes in me will never be thirsty" (6:35).

Portraying the Johannine Jesus as the incarnate wisdom of God helps to make sense of the Gospel's opening claim in 1:1 that the Word was with God (in the same way personified wisdom speaks of being beside God as a master worker), but also was God (insofar as wisdom is an aspect of God). This association of Jesus with God's Wisdom also communicates the concept of the preexistence of Jesus. This idea is unique among the canonical Gospels and one that is reiterated in the narrative. The testimony in the Prologue about Jesus being before John alludes to the idea (1:15) as does Jesus's later claim, "before Abraham was, I am" (8:58). Most explicit, however, is Jesus's prayer in 17:5: "So now, Father, glorify me in your own presence with the glory that I had in your presence before the world existed."

This close alignment with Jesus as incarnate Wisdom that was with God "in the beginning" serves to guarantee his role as the revealer of God. The audience knows from the outset that Jesus is trustworthy in what he says about God. His intimacy with God allows him to claim that his testimony is reliable—not only about God, but about himself as God's revealer. As he says to his opponents: "Even if I testify on my own behalf, my testimony is valid because I know where I have come from and where I am going" (8:14).

Finally, this association of Jesus with wisdom does something else that would not be apparent to the contemporary reader of the Gospel. By the first century CE the notion of God's Wisdom had shifted from an abstract idea of God's creative activity to an equation of Wisdom with Torah. In Jewish writings that date to the Second Temple period (around 200 BCE), God's Wisdom *is* Torah and the study of Torah is how one seeks and acquires God's Wisdom. Note this claim from the book of Baruch, for instance: "She [wisdom] is the book of the commandments of God, the law that endures forever. All who hold her fast will live, and those who forsake her will die" (Bar 4:1). The quotation from Sirach 24:19-22 included in the chart above concludes with this statement: "All this is the book of the covenant of the Most High God, the law that Moses commanded us as an inheritance for the congregations of Jacob" (Sir 24:23). This means that when the Johannine Jesus speaks as God's Wisdom, the author is implying another transfer of a central symbol in Jewish tradition, this time from a focus on Torah to a focus on Jesus. If in the past, Torah/Wisdom provided knowledge of God, now Jesus is the key to achieving such knowledge (8:19; 14:7; 17:25). The Gospel of John was not the first to make this identification. The Matthean Jesus speaks as wisdom (Matt 11:19) and presents himself as the interpreter and fulfiller of Torah (Matt 5-7; see also Luke 7:31-35). But the Gospel of John is unique in articulating such a thoroughgoing presentation of Jesus as the incarnate Wisdom of God.[16]

The Johannine Jesus as King

The title "king" is linked to Jesus sixteen times in the Gospel. The reference to Jesus as "king" frames the narrative, beginning with Nathaniel's original recognition of Jesus as "king of Israel" in 1:49 and concluding with Pilate's inscription identifying him as "King of the Jews" in 19:19-22. Much of Jesus's trial before Pilate concerns the subject of Jesus's kingship (18:33–19:3; 19:14-15). Only in this Gospel do the crowds respond to Jesus's miraculous feeding by trying to force him to become king (6:15), and only the Johannine version of Jesus's processional entry into Jerusalem has the crowd hail him as the "king of Israel" (12:12-13).

Beth Stovell shows that in addition to these explicit references to kingship associated with Jesus, many other titles and metaphors used in the Gospel add to the image of Jesus as "eternal king."[17] Being the "chosen one" recalls the chosenness of the Davidic kings (e.g., Ps 2). The "messiah," "Son of God," and "Son of Man" titles are all closely linked to notions of royalty in the Jewish tradition. As noted earlier, "Son of God" was also a typical designation for Roman emperors such as Augustus, Nero, Titus, Domitian, and Trajan.

In spite of this extensive kingship imagery, some scholars argue that the Johannine Jesus is not interested in the politics of "this world." Key to this view is an interpretation of Jesus's statement to Pilate in 18:36, "My kingdom is not from this world," as an assertion of his apolitical stance. But, as we saw in our review of empire-critical scholarship in chapter 2, recent scholarship is reconsidering the political aspects of the Gospel. To that end, Beth Stovell argues that Jesus's comment at 18:36 does *not* mean that the Johannine Jesus's reign has nothing to do with life in the first-century Roman Empire. Jesus does not say, "My kingdom is not *of* this world" as if the point was to make a spatial distinction between his heavenly kingdom and an earthly one. Instead, what Jesus says twice to Pilate is that his kingdom is not *from* this world. The point concerns the *origins* of Jesus's reigning authority. As Stovell observes, it is the source and nature of Jesus's kingdom that is in dispute, not its location. Unlike Pilate, Jesus is not granted his power and authority from the emperor and "his reign is not contingent on the desires of Rome."[18] In other words, as Warren Carter argues, "it is a mistake to assume that the emphasis on Jesus' kingship is not political . . . it is very political in that it claims to establish power over all things."[19]

The Johannine Jesus as God's Temple

According to Mary Coloe, the Gospel writer "presents the Temple as the major, consistent and pervasive symbol of Jesus' identity and mission."[20] Following the destruction of the Jerusalem temple by the Romans in 70 CE, Jewish communities struggled to find a way forward. In the absence of the sacrificial center of their tradition, the evangelist offers a solution in the person of Jesus.

Coloe points to John 2:13-25, the Johannine version of Jesus's temple action as the programmatic passage for understanding later temple imagery. In the first half of the passage, the Johannine Jesus takes up a whip of cords and drives out the animals that are there to be sold for sacrifices. He also upends the tables of the money changers and calls for an end to "making my Father's house a marketplace" (2:16).

Note that this action and Jesus's accompanying statement are more radical than what occurs in the synoptic versions. There Jesus protests against the *corruption* within the temple practice. The temple has become a "den of robbers" (Mark 11:17; Matt 21:13; Luke 19:46). But in the Gospel of John, it is the temple sacrificial system *itself* that is called into question. The buying and selling of animals for sacrifice, as well as the changing of foreign currencies for the required shekels, were regular and necessary parts of Jewish cultic practice. Nevertheless, the Johannine Jesus disrupts it and calls for its end.

There are three crucial things to keep in mind about understanding this scene. The first is to remember that the Gospel was written well after the temple had been destroyed. There are no longer any temple sacrifices happening when the Gospel writer shaped this narrative about Jesus's harsh judgment on temple practices. Second, the ancient Israelites had a long prophetic tradition of blaming national catastrophe on the Israelite people's own failures vis-à-vis God, including their sacrificial practices (see especially Isa 1:7-13). In this sense, the Johannine Jesus's actions against the temple in John 2 are in keeping with this prophetic scriptural tradition of Jewish self-critique. Third, again from within the tradition, Jesus's statement "Destroy this temple, and in three days I will raise it up" (2:19) and the narrator's explanation "he was speaking of the temple of his body"

(2:21) could be seen as a way forward after such a catastrophe. Coloe argues that this scene, written in the wake of the loss of the temple, shifts the location of God's indwelling from the Jerusalem temple to the body of Jesus. The glory of God that was once visible in Israel's tabernacle and temple (e.g., Exod 40:34) can now be seen in the Johannine Jesus (2:11).

This association of Jesus with the dwelling place of God in chapter 2 illuminates the symbolic uses of temple imagery elsewhere in the Gospel. For example, Coloe explains a puzzling comment that Jesus says to his disciples during his farewell meal by way of temple imagery. At 14:2, Jesus states, "In my Father's house there are many dwelling places. If it were not so, would I have told you that I go to prepare a place for you?" Interpreters have often understood Jesus's words as a reference to his return to heaven. But "my Father's house" is not a typical expression for heaven. Instead, in Hebrew scriptures, references to the house of God mean the Jerusalem temple. And indeed, as we have just seen, Jesus earlier refers to the temple as his "Father's house" (2:16). But if the Gospel has transferred the symbol of temple to Jesus, what does it mean to say that in Jesus there are "many dwelling places"? Here the Greek word *monai* provides a clue. It is related to the Greek verb *menō*, "to abide," which in the Johannine literature refers to an indwelling between God, Jesus, the Spirit, and the community of believers. So at the beginning of Jesus's parting words to his disciples there is a further extension of the temple theme to the community. As Coloe argues, "The Father's house will no longer be a construction of stones, but will be a *household* of many interpersonal relationships...where the divine presence can dwell within believers."[21]

Jesus as an Agent of God

The Johannine Jesus regularly describes himself as one whom God has sent into the world (3:17, 34; 5:36-38; 6:29, 57; 7:29; 8:42; 10:36; 11:42; 17:3, 21, 23, 25). Closely related to these descriptions are multiple references to Jesus's origins from heaven or from above or simply from God. Jesus tells his opposition in 8:42, "I came from God and now I am here." This is just one of several references to Jesus being "from God" (3:2; 6:46; 9:33; 13:3; 16:27). All of this suggests an otherworldly quality to the Johannine Jesus, an idea that is confirmed when he states, "I am not of this world" (8:23; see also 9:5). Again, the "of" in this phrase might be better rendered as "from" because Jesus is speaking of his origin. As an agent of God, he is sent from above into the world. Then, at the turning point of the narrative, Jesus knows that it is now the hour "to depart from this world and go to the Father" (13:1).

This pattern in the Gospel indicates that the Johannine Jesus is an emissary or "agent" of God. This latter term may sound strange to contemporary ears, but the idea of an agent being sent as a representative of an authoritative figure was common in the ancient world. Peder Borgen shows how certain aspects of Jesus's agency in the Gospel of John can be explained by what we find in legal traditions in ancient rabbinic literature.[22] For example, he argues, a main assumption in rabbinic tradition is that "the agent of the ruler is like the ruler himself." If the author of the Gospel has a similar understanding of the work of an agent, it helps to makes sense of Jesus's many claims that dealing with him is the same as dealing with God. This idea is actually found in all of the Gospels (see Mark 9:37; Matt 10:5; Luke 9:48), but it is heightened in John. When we read sayings such as "anyone who does not honor the Son does not honor the Father who sent him" (5:23), "whoever sees me sees him who sent me" (12:45), "Whoever has seen me has seen the Father" (14:9), and "If you know me, you will know my Father also" (14:7), we are seeing the Johannine Jesus express his identity as God's representative agent.

The idea of agency also incorporates the mission of the Johannine Jesus—as an obedient agent he does what is commanded by the Father (6:38).[23] William Loader builds on the idea of the Johannine Jesus as agent, calling it the "envoy revealer model." He sees Jesus's agency as part of the Gospel's christological structure. Seeing the whole of this structure, Loader contends, helps to make sense of the entire Gospel of John. Note that one can see in Loader's proposed structure below many of the key ideas we discussed as part of the Gospel's plot, or literary design:

> The Father sends and authorizes the Son, who knows the Father, comes from the Father, makes the Father known, brings light and life and truth, completes his Father's work, returns to the Father, exalted,

glorified, ascended, sends the disciples and sends the spirit to enable greater understanding, to equip for mission, and to build up the community of faith.[24]

God in the Gospel of John

Having looked at some of the core symbols connected to the Christology of the Gospel, I turn to the Johannine conception of God, as known through the Johannine Jesus. From the beginning, the Gospel points to the creative and generative aspects of God. God (with the *logos*) brings all things into being. He also "begets" his children.[25] God sends agents into the world to do his work—Jesus, of course, is sent by God, but so too is John (to testify [1:6]) and the Spirit (to testify, teach, and guide [14:26]).

God, with his Son, will "make a home with" those who love him (14:23). In this way, the Gospel writer depicts a loving God who draws people to him as part of an intimate, familial relationship. Perhaps most central to the Gospel's image of God is the following claim: "For God so loved the world that he gave his only Son, so that everyone who believes in him may not perish but may have eternal life. Indeed, God did not send the Son into the world to condemn the world, but in order that the world might be saved through him" (3:16-17).

Together, the two parts of this statement point to certain tensions that run through the Gospel. The first concerns the depiction of God in relation to the world. Here, God loves it and seeks to save the world through his Son. But in most of the rest of the Gospel the world is a hostile place. Believers are set apart from the world. Indeed, as we have already seen in the Prologue, the world did not recognize Jesus. During the farewell discourse, one of Jesus's disciples can ask: "Lord, how is it that you will reveal yourself to us, and not to the world?" (14:22). Likewise, Jesus can assure his disciples that they do not belong to the world: "If the world hates you, be aware that it hated me before it hated you. If you belonged to the world, the world would love you as its own. Because you do not belong to the world, but I have chosen you out of the world—therefore the world hates you" (15:18-19).

Perhaps the problem of contrasts in references to the "world" in the Gospel comes from the fact that this term functions in different ways at different points. We already saw a similar phenomenon at the end of the previous chapter in the different ways that "the Jews" (*hoi Iudaioi*) functions at different points in the Gospel, sometimes in neutral or positive ways, but more often serving the dualistic worldview of the Gospel. Therefore, John 3:16 can assert that "God so loved the world" even as other parts of the Gospel insist that the world is an inhospitable place, that its ruler opposes God and God's children (14:30; 16:11), and this means that believers are hated and can expect persecution (15:19-20).

The second tension concerns the ideas of God in relation to judgment. We have already seen the conflicting statements concerning Jesus as one who judges. In 3:17, the idea of God's role in condemnation is refuted. God does not send his Son to condemn the world. Nevertheless, there is judgement, as the very next verse shows: "those who do not believe are condemned already, because they have not believed in the name of the only Son of God" (3:18). This tension is also evident in places where the author retains a traditional notion of God as an eschatological judge, that is, one who judges the righteous and the unrighteous on the "last day." This future judgment is suggested in 5:29, where Jesus speaks of a "resurrection to condemnation" and at 12:48, where the word that Jesus has spoken will be a judge on the last day (see also 6:39-40). But in other cases, such as 3:18, the idea of judgment shifts entirely to the present. Moreover, it does not seem to be God who judges, but rather a sort of self-condemnation that takes place. Notice in the following verse how there is no subject who judges, but simply "the judgment," one that is based on the fact that people loved darkness. "And this is the judgment, that the light has come into the world, and people loved darkness rather than light because their deeds were evil" (3:19).

Similarly, the Johannine Jesus can speak of coming "for judgment" but not necessarily "to judge." Again, the idea of recognition on the part of those who encounter Jesus seems to be the key.[26] "Jesus said, 'I came into this world for judgment so that those who do not see may see, and those who do see may become blind' " (9:39).

Assuming that one does "see" Jesus, that is, recognize who he is and who sent him, what can one expect? Most often, the answer given in the Gospel is "eternal life."

Salvation as "Eternal Life"

In the Greek version of the Gospel the expression that is translated as *eternal life* appears fifteen times, with *life* also appearing on its own at many points. The meaning of the phrase is a difficult concept for readers to grasp since at first glance it might seem to mean living forever. And in fact, the Johannine Jesus does say that those who eat the bread and water that he offers will never die (4:13-14; 6:50-51). But, he also explains to Martha, "I am the resurrection and the life. Those who believe in me, even though they die, will live" (11:25). Clearly, eternal life does not mean the end of physical death. Perhaps the most helpful statement for understanding what eternal life means in the Gospel comes in chapter 10. There the Johannine Jesus explains, "I came that they may have life, and have it abundantly" (10:10). This full life is key to the notion of eternal life in the Gospel. This abundance may be expressed symbolically in the large quantity of wine that Jesus produces for his first sign (2:6-7), as well as in the oversupply of food that Jesus provides for the crowd of five thousand people (6:13). These material examples point to the notion of the *quality* of life that Jesus promises for those who know God. In fact, Jesus defines eternal life in his prayer as knowing God: "And this is eternal life, that they may know you, the only true God, and Jesus Christ whom you have sent" (17:3).

And while this eternal life does not mean avoiding physical death, the abundant aspect of it does imply a transcendent existence that continues after one's physical life. The Johannine Jesus does not speak about this as a life somewhere up in heaven. Nearly every time the word *heaven* appears in the Gospel, it is in reference to either Jesus or gifts from God having come from heaven. And in fact, the narrator claims that "no one has ascended into heaven except the one who descended from heaven, the Son of Man" (3:13). To be sure one must be born from above, or born of water and the spirit, to see and enter God's reign (3:3, 5), but this too does not indicate *going to* someplace as much as *existing in* a new relationship with God. Because this relationship begins with belief, it is available in the present.

One other image may help illumine this idea of "eternal life," though it comes from the book of *Revelation*, a New Testament book that is conceptually related to the Johannine literature. At the end of this book, the salvation from God is imagined as a gleaming new Jerusalem and new temple *coming down* from heaven. The result is described this way: "See, the home of God is among mortals. He will dwell with them; they will be his peoples, and God himself will be with them" (Rev 21:3). This language of mutual dwelling between God and his people includes light imagery similar to the Gospel. "And there will be no more night; they need no light of lamp or sun, for the Lord God will be their light, and they will reign forever and ever" (Rev 22:5). In a similar way, the eternal life that the Gospel promises the community of believers is a "forever and ever" abiding in love with God and God's Son.

Finally, Jesus describes the salvation he brings in terms of joy (15:11; 16:24) and peace (14:27; 16:33; 20:19, 21). Such language is not unusual for the ancient world. Both Jewish and Greco-Roman writings anticipate and long for a time of joy and peace ushered in by a new age. Again, the Johannine Jesus suggests that this new age is already present: "Very truly, I tell you, anyone who hears my word and believes him who sent me has eternal life, and does not come under judgment, but has passed from death to life" (5:24).

What such a life involves on a daily basis is not specified. But the theological promise of the Gospel is that life in community with Jesus, God, and fellow believers will bring a joy that is complete (15:11; 16:24; 17:13).

The Meaning of the Death of the Johannine Jesus

Because Jesus repeatedly states that believing in him is the necessary element to be born into this new life, another puzzle presents itself. What is the meaning and significance of Jesus's death in relation to salvation? This has been the subject of much scholarly debate, and here I will just point to the distinctive aspects of the Gospel regarding the death of Jesus.

First, Jesus's death is not portrayed as a necessary suffering that must occur as it is in the Gospel of Mark (8:31; 9:31). Rather, the death of the Johannine Jesus is referred to as a "lifting up" (3:14-15) and repeatedly as the hour of Jesus's glorification (12:23-24; 13:1). For this reason, some have suggested that Jesus's death is merely the necessary means for Jesus's return to his place of glory alongside the Father.

But, there is more to the depiction of the Johannine Jesus's death than that. The author portrays it as a unifying act. When the Greeks go to the Passover festival and look for Jesus, he takes it as an indication that the hour of his glorification has come (12:20-23). Soon after, the Gospel relates a statement by Jesus along with its interpretation. "And I, when I am lifted up from the earth, will draw all people to myself. He said this to indicate the kind of death he was to die" (12:32-33).

More difficult is the question of whether the Gospel writer sees the death of Jesus as a sacrificial death, especially a sacrifice of atonement. There is little explicit language in the Gospel to support this view. Even if Jesus "takes away the sin of the world" (1:29), there is no indication that God requires his death to atone for the sin in the world. In the Gospel of John, the death of Jesus seems necessary not for atonement but to usher in the next stage in the life of the community. Note how Jesus metaphorically explains his impending death: "The hour has come for the Son of Man to be glorified. Very truly, I tell you, unless a grain of wheat falls into the earth and dies, it remains just a single grain; but if it dies, it bears much fruit" (12:23-24).

This fruit-bearing death points ahead to the fruit-bearing community that will "abide in him" when he is gone (see 15:1-5). Similarly, Jesus tells his disciples that they will benefit if he goes, because only in this way can the "Advocate" come to them (16:7).

Moreover, the Gospel does not focus on the necessary aspect of Jesus's death as much as it does the voluntary nature of his death. In fact, in the same discourse that the Johannine Jesus speaks of coming to give life abundantly, he also refers to laying down his life (10:15). In so doing he emphasizes that no one is taking his life; he offers it on his own accord (10:18). As we discuss in the next chapter, such a death fits within a tradition of noble death in the ancient world. One dies nobly precisely when one willingly dies on behalf of another, or on behalf of a cause. The Greek formula for this dying "on behalf of" (*hyper*) occurs several times with respect to the death of Jesus. It appears twice with respect to Caiaphas's ironic prediction that Jesus died for the people (11:50; 18:14). It is also used twice by Jesus with respect to laying down his life for his sheep (10:15) and his friends (15:30). This type of noble death is what brings glory in the ancient world.

The Question of Ecclesiology and Ethics in the Fourth Gospel

Although much of the historical scholarship on the Gospel is centered on the idea of a particular Johannine community, rarely do scholars refer to this group as the "Johannine church." Indeed, some have argued that the author shows little interest in ecclesiology, that is, in matters pertaining to the institution of the church. It is true that *ecclesia*, the Greek word for assembly or church, does not appear in the Johannine literature. Nor do we find the type of ecclesial traditions that we see in the Gospel of Matthew where Jesus speaks of building his church (Matt 16:18) and gives instructions for navigating conflict among church members (Matt 18:15-22). Contrasting with the Gospel of Luke, the writer of this Gospel does not situate the story of Jesus and his followers as part of a longer history of God's saving acts. Unlike in the book of Acts, we find no sense of a spreading movement to bring salvation "to the ends of the earth" (Acts 1:8; 13:47; note also the strong missionary outreach of Matt 28:19-20). There is also an absence of traditions related to the institution of the sacraments. There is no depiction of Jesus's baptism in the Gospel (cp. Mark 1:9-11; Matt 3:13-17; Luke 3:21-22) and no institution of the Eucharist at a Passover meal with the disciples (cp. Mark 14:22-25; Matt 26:26-29; Luke 22:15-20).

But these details only confirm what we already know. The Gospel of John approaches the traditions about Jesus in a very different way than do the Synoptic Gospels. The same is true about how it portrays the community of believers. While there is no reference to a church, there are certainly images of the communal nature of Jesus's followers.

For example, in 10:1-16, Jesus uses pastoral metaphors to evoke a sense of belonging—believers are the flock whom Jesus, as shepherd, leads, protects, and defends (cf. 10:3-4, 9-15). This sense of communal life is strengthened in the farewell discourse of chapters 14–17. There Jesus speaks metaphorically of the integral relationship between God, Jesus, and his followers. God is the vine grower, Jesus is the vine, and his followers are branches. Only by remaining on the vine, "abiding in" Jesus, is the community able to bear fruit (5:1-5). This image also includes the idea of mutual "abiding" or "remaining with" that is an essential feature of the Johannine vision of the believing community. As we saw in the discussion of Jesus as the new dwelling place for God, he promises his followers: "I will come again and will take you to myself, so that where I am, there you may be also" (14:3).

This reference to "bearing fruit" suggests that there are particular expectations for conduct in the community, even though what "bearing fruit" looks like is not detailed. There are also hints of the sort of apostolic outreach that Jesus commissions in Matthew and Luke. Earlier in the Gospel, the Johannine Jesus refers to a sending of his disciples to build on the earlier work of others (4:38). During his farewell speech, he instructs them to bear witness to him after he is gone (15:27). Even more, in his post-resurrection appearance to the disciples, Jesus offers himself as a model, this time extending his own "sentness" to them: "'Peace be with you. As the Father has sent me, so I send you.' When he had said this, he breathed on them and said to them, 'Receive the Holy Spirit'" (20:21-22).

The Johannine disciples are not sent to make other disciples "of all nations" as in Matthew (28:19). But, they are "sent" as Jesus was "sent," suggesting that they are to continue his earthly mission after he is gone. This notion is confirmed by the Johannine Jesus's earlier prediction about his followers: "Very truly, I tell you, the one who believes in me will also do the works that I do and, in fact, will do greater works than these, because I am going to the Father (14:12). The audience is not told what these "greater works" will be. If they are modeled on the Johannine Jesus, they might include healing, feeding, or indeed, revealing God to the world. Finally, similar to the commission in the Gospel of Luke, the Johannine Jesus tells the disciples that they have the ability to forgive or to retain the sins of others (20:23; cf. Luke 24:47). Yet the Johannine Jesus has not spoken earlier of repentance or forgiveness (though this is a common theme in the Gospel of Luke), making this a somewhat perplexing description of the disciples' mission in the world. Most likely it is another way of indicating that the disciples now have the authority to carry on the work of Jesus in the world.

The giving of the Holy Spirit to the disciples at this point is an additional indication that Jesus's hour of glorification has occurred (see 7:39). It also highlights a distinctive aspect of communal life for Jesus's followers. During his words of departure, Jesus promises that a *paraklētos* will be sent to them. In some English translations, this Greek term is left untranslated as "Paraclete" (as in the NJB). This is because it is difficult to settle on a corresponding English word. The word literally means something like "one called beside," whether in a legal sense as an advocate, or simply as one who lends aid or support. All of these meanings make sense at the various places where *paraklētos* occurs. Thus *paraklētos* is often translated as "advocate," as in the NRSV, or "helper" (NASB), or "comforter" (KJV), or even "companion" (CEB). In the following description, *paraklētos* is used interchangeably with the Holy Spirit, while also seeming to refer to a specific person who will guide the community after Jesus is gone: "But the Advocate, the Holy Spirit, whom the Father will send in my name, will teach you everything, and remind you of all that I have said to you" (14:26).

Part of the difficulty with speaking about a Johannine ethics is that the language related to the community in the Gospel is decidedly inward looking. The Gospel repeatedly defines the followers of Jesus as those who abide in his love in contrast to those of the world who do not. If we turn to the question of ethics, this in-group dynamic presents some serious difficulties, especially when measured against the Synoptic Gospels. In the latter, it is easy to find instructions for a moral life that reach beyond relationships between the followers of Christ. In the Gospel of Luke, Jesus uses the parable of the Good Samaritan to expand the definition of neighbor beyond one's own community (Luke 10:29-37). In both the Gospels of Matthew and Luke, Jesus instructs his listeners to love their enemies (Matt 5:44; Luke 6:27). Both feature the famous golden rule to treat others in the way you would like to be treated (Matt 7:12; Luke 6:31). Meanwhile, the Johannine Jesus speaks only in general terms of obeying the commandments and offers only one specific instruction: "This is my commandment, that you love one another as I have loved you" (15:12).

Especially in light of the admonitions given by the Matthean and Lukan Jesus that it is easy to love someone who loves you—even tax collectors and sinners manage that (Matt 5:46; Luke 6:32)—the Johannine Jesus's command to direct one's love toward others in the community is striking. One can understand Wayne Meeks's assertion that one cannot truly speak of an ethical vision in the Gospel of John. In addition to noting the Gospel's lack of explicit moral instruction, Meeks suggests that the Johannine Jesus's manner of communicating "by riddle, metaphor, irony, and double entendre" does not provide the means for a rational ethical discourse. Finally, he points to what we observed in the last chapter about Johannine characters. They are not morally free actors who can choose what side of the divide they find themselves on. Those chosen out of the world can only make the right choice, and those who are not chosen cannot.

To be sure, one perhaps can paint Johannine ethics in broad strokes. Followers of Jesus are to obey the commandments, just as Jesus obeyed the commandments (15:10). Nevertheless, the dualistic nature of the Gospel makes it difficult to look past the binary division between the children of God and the children of the devil. Indeed, as we will discuss in the next chapter, once the Gospel moves beyond its first-century setting, certain interpretations have tended to generate more ethical problems than solve them.

Is the Gospel of John Supersessionist?

Having come to the end of this discussion of Johannine theology, we come to a painful topic for the history of Jewish and Christian relations.

Supersessionism is the belief that God's new covenant with followers of Christ replaces God's ancient covenant with Israel. To ask whether the Gospel is supersessionist is to ask if it presents Jesus and his followers as superior to and replacing Judaism and its adherents in God's eyes.

This is a question related to the Gospel's depiction of "the Jews" as opponents of Jesus, but it involves other aspects of the Gospel as well. We have seen how the Christology of the Gospel draws on traditions that were of central importance to the Jewish tradition. One way of understanding these symbols is to situate them in the wake of the trauma of the destruction of the temple by Rome in 70 CE. With the temple destroyed, Judaism had to find a way to continue without its ritual center. One could read Johannine Christology as firmly embedded in the Jewish tradition, expressing all of its deepest hopes and convictions in the person of Jesus. In this sense, Jesus becomes the eternal king of Israel, the locus of the indwelling of God among people, the heavenly agent who mediates God to the world, and indeed, God's own wisdom. All of these associations could be seen as ways of expressing that God was still present with his people in Jesus, even after the destruction of the temple. Beyond this, the Prologue distinguishes the gift of the law from Moses with the gift of grace from Jesus (1:18). Philip describes Jesus as the one "about whom Moses in the law and also the prophets wrote" (1:45). The Gospel includes claims that the Jewish ancestors and prophets—Abraham (8:56), Moses (5:46), Isaiah (12:38-41)—knew of him and anticipated his coming.

As long as this was a conversation taking place within Judaism, it could be viewed as one proposal among several about how Judaism could continue in a post-temple world. In this context, the Gospel of John might not stand as an attempt to supersede Judaism, but instead as a proposal for how Jewish tradition would best survive. After all, following the temple's destruction, it was not clear which Jewish groups would succeed in defining the shape of a post-temple Judaism. Many followers of Jesus, even Gentile followers, saw themselves as part of a historical Jewish tradition with roots in the Torah, temple, and promises of the Hebrew scriptures.

Nevertheless, once the followers of Jesus understood themselves to be part of a *separate* tradition called Christianity that was distinct from

Judaism, the significance of the Gospel's depiction of Jesus in relation to Judaism would dramatically shift.

Scholars debate about exactly when and how the separation of Christianity and Judaism happened. Once it did, however, the depiction of the Johannine Jesus and "the Jews" took on a supersessionist meaning. Within this context of increasingly non-Jewish "Christianity" the readers saw in the Gospel (and other New Testament writings) a condemnation of Judaism and an endorsement of Jesus as a replacement for central Jewish symbols: temple, Torah, the messiah, and so on. The ongoing challenge for Christians now is to define Christianity in positive ways rather than over against, and at the expense of, its parent tradition.

Chapter 5

Exploring Ideology in the Gospel of John

So far, this book has introduced you to the Gospel of John by way of historical, literary, and theological approaches to the text. The goal of these approaches is to explain the meaning of the text. This could be the meaning of the text as it was intended by its first-century author (historical criticism), the meaning of the text as conveyed by the narrative (literary criticism), or the meaning of the text with respect to what it says about God, Jesus, and the community of believers (theological perspectives).

Ideological approaches to the Bible have a different goal. This type of scholarship attempts to make explicit how certain ideas contained in biblical texts or in the interpretations of biblical texts may contribute to social, political, and economic injustices. Ideological critics begin with the theory that because all texts are produced in particular times and places, they all will be shaped in some way by particular convictions or assumptions about the world. These "ideologies" are related to power. Ideological critics explore how knowledge is produced and spread, and how this knowledge builds and reinforces the power of certain groups and institutions. One such way of producing knowledge is through literature. Thus, ideological critics often study literary texts. They read between the lines, below the surface, and often against the grain of a particular writing to discover its implicit ideologies and underlying power structures.

While you may find some of the scholarly perspectives in this chapter to be challenging, I include them here because (1) they constitute a significant part of contemporary scholarship on the Gospel and (2) they offer a crucial component of reading the Bible responsibly. This second point is no less true—indeed it may be especially true—for communities for whom the Bible has scriptural authority.

We have already seen an example of why this is so. In both the historical and literary readings of the Gospel discussed earlier, we studied the negative portrayal of a group referred to as "the Jews" in the Gospel. Biblical critics using historical criticism have attempted to explain this portrayal by positing a synagogue expulsion behind the Gospel's heated rhetoric. Scholars using literary criticism have studied "the Jews" as a character group that represents unbelief, or the collective voice of opposition against Jesus. None of these approaches fully addresses the problems posed by having such language in Christian scripture. In a case like this, ideological criticism of the portrayal of "the Jews" in John can help us recognize, for example, the dangerous implications of accepting the Johannine Jesus's labeling of "the Jews" as children of the devil. As a result of centuries of anti-Judaism and especially the Nazi genocide of Jews, we now know the potential fatal consequences of such words. Thus we no longer can accept anti-Jewish statements, even in a biblical Gospel, at face value. Ideological criticism would challenge interpretations that accept, or even excuse, such anti-Jewish language.

Ideological approaches tend to be eclectic. Indeed, one should think of the term "ideological criticism" as an umbrella that encompasses a range of approaches that read with an eye toward how the text implicitly supports (or opposes) unjust or otherwise damaging social structures: patriarchy, racism, colonialism, homophobia, and so on. In this chapter, I discuss analyses of the Gospel that are grounded in feminist theory, gender theory, masculinity studies, queer theory, and postcolonial theory. What they have in common is an interest in reading for justice for those who have been treated with injustice.

Feminist Criticism and Roles of Women in the Gospel of John

The Johannine Jesus and Women

Read: 2:4; 4:21; 19:26; 20:15. What do these texts have in common? Is there something similar in these depictions of Jesus speaking with women that links the scenes together thematically?

The verses listed above recall what we already noticed in chapter 2. The Johannine Jesus converses with individual characters throughout the Gospel. But they show something more. In many cases the Johannine Jesus converses with individual women. The number of these encounters is remarkable in itself, especially compared to the lack of many such dialogues in the Synoptic Gospels. The Johannine Jesus speaks with his mother (2:3-4), then with an unnamed Samaritan woman (4:7-26), then with Martha of Bethany (11:20-27), and finally, with Mary Magdalene (20:14-17). Perhaps this does not seem odd for a twenty-first-century reader, but in the ancient Mediterranean culture, unrelated women and men did not meet and talk together. Notice that at one point the Gospel writer even signals how unusual this type of encounter would seem to onlookers. In 4:27, when the disciples return to Jesus, they are "astonished that he was speaking with a woman, but no one said, 'What do you want?' or, 'Why are you speaking with her?'" The disciples, though surprised at Jesus's actions, do not ask him to explain himself. Note also that the Johannine Jesus calls attention to the gender of his conversation partners by repeatedly addressing them with the Greek term *gynai*, meaning "woman." The designation is used even for his own mother. Taken together, these observations suggest that the category of "woman" is in some way significant to the Johannine narrative. But how?

The first attempts to answer this question occurred in the midst of the women's movement of the 1970s when feminist biblical criticism emerged. Feminist criticism is a type of ideological criticism focused on challenging injustices against women. One main goal of feminist critics of the Bible is to uncover the way the biblical text or interpretations of the biblical text reinforce gender stereotypes. Some feminist interpreters propose alternative ways of reading without a gender bias.

In past decades, feminist criticism of the Gospel of John has taken several forms. Early feminist critics of the Gospel focused on the history of a Johannine community, arguing that female characters in the Gospel reflect a historical situation where women held prominent roles in the community. Sandra Schneiders, for example, concludes that the prominence of women in the Gospel is difficult to understand unless women were actually leaders in the Johannine community. Similarly, she reads the disciples' questioning of Jesus in 4:27 as evidence of a controversy within the community where some male members were likely shocked by the "independence and apostolic initiative of Christian women."[1]

Once literary criticism emerged, feminist scholars focused on the role of women in the narrative. From this perspective, female characters appear to be associated with key moments of revelation in the Gospel. The mother of Jesus is linked to Jesus's first sign where Jesus reveals his glory to his disciples (2:4-11), the conversation with the Samaritan woman leads to Jesus's self-revelation as the messiah (4:25-26), and his encounter with Martha of Bethany includes his revelation as "the resurrection and the life" (11:25-27). Mary Magdalene is the first to encounter the risen Jesus (20:14-16), and she is the first to communicate this news to the male disciples (20:17-18).[2]

Here I should note that the focus of many of the early studies of roles of women in the Gospel were focused on the question of equality. These studies asked whether the women in the Gospel are depicted as sharing equal status with the male disciples. Meanwhile, none of the early studies that examined the function of women as *women* in the Gospel also looked at the Gospel's portrayal of men as *men*. The assumption seemed to be that the female characters in the Gospel should be measured against the standard set by the male disciples (hence the question of whether women were "equal" to the male disciples). This assumption changed with the introduction of gender as an analytic category in the humanities. Gender

critics argue that both "woman" *and* "man" are culturally constructed categories, as are the adjectives "feminine" and "masculine." What it means
to be a "man" or "woman" varies between different historical periods and
different cultural settings. Gender critics also assert that gender categories
are constructed in relation to one another. One can only study what it
means to be a woman in relation to what it means to be a man, and vice
versa. For the study of the Gospel of John, this means that both men and
women needed to be examined in the narrative.

A look at these questions from a literary perspective shows that women
in the Gospel often play a *more* prominent role than comparable male
characters at key places in the narrative. To return to the scenes mentioned
above, the mother of Jesus acts as a catalyst for Jesus's first sign (2:3-5),
which then brings the male disciples to belief (2:11). After Jesus reveals
himself to the Samaritan woman, she then witnesses to her people about
him and many are brought to belief because of her (4:26-30, 39). Martha,
not Peter, offers a full and unequivocal confession of faith in Jesus that
corresponds to the express purpose of the Gospel (11:27; cf. 20:31; Mark
8:29; Matt 16:16; Luke 9:20). Mary Magdalene, not Peter or the beloved
disciple, is the first to witness the post-resurrection Jesus and to witness to
the male disciples (20:11-18).

On the other hand, one cannot neatly divide the Gospel's revelation
and recognition scenes down gender lines. As we saw in our study of Johannine characters, the man born blind in chapter 9 is brought to belief
on the basis of Jesus's self-revelation and offers his own confession of faith
(9:37-38). And of course, the beloved disciple shares a place of intimacy
with the Johannine Jesus that is matched only by Jesus's own intimate position vis-à-vis God (13:23, cp. 1:18). Both of these male characters stand
apart from the tradition of the twelve male disciples. It may be that the
Gospel writer wanted to distance the Johannine Jesus from the figures of
authority that were emerging in the Christian tradition.

Moreover, the example of the man born blind, in particular, points to
the problem of reading Johannine women as representative of historical
women who held leadership positions. The logic of reading characters as
stand-ins for actual historical figures means that we would need to assume

117

that this unnamed formerly blind man represents a formerly blind man who held a leadership position in the hypothetical community. In light of this positive depiction of outsider male disciples and of women, we gain new perspective on the use of female gender in the Gospel. Female characters are not reflections of prominent female figures in the Johannine community any more than that community prominently featured men who had been born blind. Rather, the significance of female characters (along with the man born blind and the beloved disciple) may be their non-traditional quality. The implications of this interpretation are nearly the opposite of the "equality" argument. If the author does not want to feature the traditional figures of the authority in the church (as in the tradition of the twelve male disciples), it may be women's culturally determined role as *subordinate, non-authoritative* women that make them appealing choices as conversation partners for the Johannine Jesus.[3]

Whatever the reasons for the Gospel's focus on female characters, these insights from gender-critical analysis of the Gospel show that the ancient author probably was not concerned about the equality of women. Although occasionally Roman writers discuss the capacity of women to act in virtuous ways, they consider women to be acting like men in such cases. And in the rare cases where authors advocate for the education of women, the point is not that women and men are equal and thus equally deserving of education, but rather that women who are educated can better fulfill the duties befitting a woman.

Symbolic Uses of Gender in John

There is more to the study of gender analysis of the Gospel than simply assessing the function of characters in the narrative. It also involves study of its gendered metaphorical and symbolic language. What are the implications of calling God "Father," for example? And what is the significance of calling the Johannine Jesus "God's only begotten Son"? Because these phrases use metaphorical language, they are inherently open to interpretation. Here the setting and purpose of particular feminist readings play a role in how the Gospel is viewed. Feminist scholars who interpret the Bible within and for the Christian community are typically interested in interpretations that both empower women in the church and resist gender bias. As Dorothy Lee states, her concern is to read by way of the "evangelical purpose of the Gospel—and its purpose within the church's canon ...the transformation of real readers within the contemporary world."[4]

Feminist scholars who interpret the Bible in light of its ancient cultural context often show how androcentrism and patriarchy have contributed to the symbolism of the Gospel. One could argue that their goal is also transformation, but it is not a transformation that is neatly aligned with the evangelical purpose of the Gospel. Rather, these interpretations aim for the type of cognitive transformation that occurs with understanding how certain cultural texts (like the Gospel of John) reflect and contribute to the power structures of the world. Both types of scholarship have important contributions to make. Below I show this by reviewing different scholarly assessments of three aspects of the Gospel: (1) the use of father/son language for God/Jesus; (2) the use of wisdom symbolism; and (3) the metaphors of birth and begetting.

Jesus, Gender, and Personified Wisdom

As we saw in the last chapter, there are a number of ways that the Gospel presents Jesus as the incarnate wisdom of God. Feminist scholars seeking a feminine dimension of the divine in the Gospel often turn first to this aspect of Johannine Christology. Recall that in Jewish scriptural traditions, God's wisdom is often personified as a female figure (see chapter 4). One reason for this is that the word for *wisdom* is feminine (*hokma* in Hebrew, *sophia* in Greek). Although others have recognized Wisdom motifs in the Gospel, reading from a gender-critical perspective produces a different type of assessment of this language. For example, Martin Scott argues both that Johannine Christology is *primarily* influenced by the figure of Sophia and that the Gospel writer realized the problem of linking a female figure to the male person of Jesus. This is why, according to Scott, the evangelist introduced the masculine term *logos*. As we saw in the last chapter, Hellenistic Jewish writers like Philo sometimes used *logos* as an equivalent term for God's wisdom. In Scott's view, the masculine word *logos* satisfies "both the requirements of the *maleness* of the human Jesus and the *equivalence* to the female Sophia."[5] With this observation, Martin is able to find gender inclusivity in the presentation of the Johannine Jesus. "The point of John's wisdom Christology," he argues, "is precisely that Jesus Sophia is not mere man but the incarnation of both the male and female expressions of the divine, albeit within the limitations of human flesh."[6]

Scott is not alone in finding a feminine dimension in the Gospel by way of wisdom imagery. Other scholars see wisdom imagery as bringing a feminine aspect to the Gospel because of maternal associations. According to J. Massyngbaerde Ford, Wisdom's call to eat and drink is suggestive of the nourishing role of the mother, and this extends to the Johannine Jesus's use of similar language.[7] Dorothy Lee agrees and also points to another reason that Wisdom traditions in the Bible may be personified as female. Scholars have long seen parallels between the wisdom language in the Bible and the Egyptian-Hellenistic goddess Isis. If so, this goddess language would have indirectly influenced the wisdom traditions in the Gospel. Lee notes especially the portrayal of Isis as "a figure of divine sovereignty...maternal and authoritative, possessing dominion over the whole creation including the power of life and death."[8] All of these scholars seek a feminine dimension in the Gospel in an effort to show the gender inclusivity of the Gospel.

But there is a contrasting view. Although most scholars recognize the Gospel's use of Wisdom traditions, some do not see this as evidence of a feminine aspect in the text. Consider Wayne Meeks's claim that "there is no trace of the usual feminine Sophia" in the Gospel's evocation of the masculine *logos*, "she has become entirely the masculine Logos, the Son of Man."[9] Far from seeing the Gospel writer as introducing *logos* as a way of incorporating feminine Sophia, Meeks sees it as a way of obscuring any trace of it. Feminist scholar Elizabeth Schüssler Fiorenza comes to a similar conclusion. She argues that (1) because the Gospel so frequently uses "Son" as a designation for Jesus and (2) because the incarnation equates God's *logos* with the biological sex of the male Jesus, the Gospel effectively "marginalizes and silences the traditions of G*d as represented by Divine Woman wisdom."[10] These latter interpretations are offered not as a way of oppressing women, but as a way of taking seriously the strongly masculine language of the text. In this sense, they provide a caution to overly optimistic views of the presence of the divine feminine in the Gospel.[11]

God the Father and Jesus the Son

Our second example concerns precisely the masculine language I just mentioned. The Gospel writer uses the metaphorical designations of father and son for God and Jesus more often than any other metaphor. By my count, Father appears 113 times as a designation for God, and Jesus is referred to as Son (including Son of God, Son of Man, and son of Joseph) 47 times. Reading from a feminist theological perspective, some scholars argue that it is a mistake to interpret these metaphors as androcentric. According to Gail O'Day, for example, the Gospel neither reinforces patriarchy nor promotes the male gender. Instead, the meaning of the metaphor lies in the intimate relationship it expresses. As she puts it, "Jesus calls God father in John in order to evoke a new world in which intimate, loving relations with God and one another are possible."[12] Dorothy Lee comes to a similar conclusion. Like O'Day, Lee cites the quality of intimacy that exists between father and son that is based in a loving relationship that draws others into the same. She notes that "all are invited...to share the same love...that Jesus possesses with the Father."[13] Moreover, according to Lee the symbol of the Johannine Father is concerned with the surrender or giving away of power. The sending of the Son by the Father represents God's gift to the world, which she suggests is God's own self. She writes, "It is a costly and vulnerable sending, given through death."[14] In her view, these aspects of the Gospel "seriously destabilize paternalistic models."

Lee offers this interpretation by focusing on the symbolic world within the text. But if we consider the world in which the text was written, such male-oriented language for figures of divine authority are in keeping with the androcentric and patriarchal culture in which the Gospel was written. Roman family law gave the father ultimate power over the lives of the children and slaves in his household as well as their descendants. This power of the father is also reflected in one of the titles adopted by the Roman emperor. He was *patria patriae*, "father of the fatherland." Thus, from a cultural perspective, referring to God as a father who gives authority to his son reinforces the ideology of male dominion and power. Indeed, some feminist critics see these masculine metaphors for the divine as dangerous projections of a male-dominated culture and society onto a cosmic screen. Such projections have the potential to reinforce all the more the limitations for women inherent in androcentric cultures and institutions.

Maternal and Birth Imagery in the Gospel of John

As part of her work on gender and symbolism in the Gospel, Lee traces what she sees as an extensive network of maternal imagery that complements the more dominant father imagery. This network includes both explicit and implicit references to birth. Explicitly, the Johannine Jesus speaks of the need to be born anew of the spirit and from above (3:3, 7-8). When comforting his disciples about his departure, the Johannine Jesus uses the example of a woman's experience of labor and delivery as an analogy for the pain and joy the disciples will feel at his departure and then return (16:21-22).

As part of the network of maternal symbols, Lee also offers a unique reading of the scene at the foot of the cross featuring the mother of Jesus and the beloved disciple (19:26-27). She first notes that it makes narrative sense for Jesus to offer the beloved disciple as a replacement for the son she is about to lose. But why, Lee asks, does his disciple need a replacement mother? Lee argues that the only conclusion is that "Here is your mother" implies that he is offering his mother as a replacement for his own presence. "*Jesus himself in his earthly ministry has been the 'mother' to the Beloved Disciple*" (italics original).[15] Lee continues this reading of Jesus as mother by finding birth imagery in the flow of water and blood from Jesus's side (19:31-37). The symbolism links with earlier references to water and birth in the narrative. "Jesus' death is presented as the sorrowful labor that brings forth the joy of life (16:21); his wounded side is also the *koilia*, the womb that produces life."[16]

In direct contrast to seeing birth language in the Gospel as metaphorically pointing to the presence of a maternal, feminine dimension, both Adele Reinhartz and Turid Karlsen Seim make a case for its masculine connotations. Reinhartz shows that in the ancient setting of the Gospel the "begetting" terminology in the Gospel would correspond to the *male* generative role. Moreover, it would do so in a literal way. Her argument is based on the quite limited understanding of the human reproductive process at the time, especially as seen in Aristotle's widely known ideas regarding the reproducing process.

Aristotle's reproductive theory reflects the ancient gender ideology that defined masculinity as the active, creative force in nature. Reinhartz finds echoes of Aristotle in the Gospel's Prologue, which contains a cluster of vocabulary that is also found in Aristotle's theory of reproduction.[17] For example, according to Aristotle, the male seed (*logos*) provides both the form and creative activity for reproduction. It carries the *pneuma* (the male life-breath) that provides the potential form of the offspring. The female provides the material.[18] Reinhartz suggests that if the author of the Gospel had a general sense of this theory (and its prevalence in the ancient world makes this quite possible), the repeated reference to Jesus "coming from" God may be a *literal* reference to his being begotten from divine male seed. Reinhartz finds additional support for her interpretation in 1 John 3:9, "Those who have been born of God do not sin, because God's seed abides in them; they cannot sin, because they have been born of God." This generative process of a divine seed coming from God the Father then extends also to believers who become children of God (John 1:13).

Note that Reinhartz's interpretation has implications for how one understands the father/son language in the Gospel. Again, her work suggests that in its ancient context this language may not have been a metaphorical expression, but a *literal* indication of the generative link between God and Jesus. To that end, Reinhartz also points to another curious and unexplained aspect of the Gospel. In several places, the Gospel seems to distance the Johannine Jesus from his mother. In contrast to the many references to God as Father, Jesus refers to his mother only as "woman" (2:4; 19:26). In her first appearance, Jesus's comment to her—literally, "What to me and to you, woman?"—is an idiomatic found in the Hebrew scriptures that indicates a distancing, if not a rebuke to one who is bothering another (e.g., Judg 11:12; 1 Kings 17:18; 2 Kings 3:13). Moreover, in the Gospel of John, the mother of Jesus (who is never called Mary) appears in the Gospel only at the beginning and end of his ministry.

Turid Karsen Seim explores more fully the implications of Reinhartz's work for the presentation of the Johannine Jesus's mother. She asks, "Does Jesus' mother in John have a place also in the discourse of divine origin and begetting from above?"[19] The question is necessary since it is *Jesus* who takes on the generative role, according to Seim. His exaltation signals "the process of giving birth from above to children begotten of God."[20] Seim concludes that his mother serves at the cross as a reminder of Jesus's embodiment. She relates to his "story in the flesh" but little more. This interpretation stands in stark contrast to those, like Lee, who associate the Gospel's birth language with a maternal role. Seim reminds the reader that in the ancient Greco-Roman world "giving birth was not necessarily giving life" because life came from the father. Overall, she concludes that "there is no female principle involved in the divine begetting and birth giving."[21]

Greco-Roman Masculinities and the Johannine Jesus

Beyond the study of symbols and metaphorical language in the Gospel, there is another way to analyze gender in relation to the Johannine Jesus. This is to compare the way he is depicted in the Gospel with what other contemporary Greco-Roman writers had to say about being a true man. In the past few decades, a number of studies of classical writers have provided detailed descriptions of what it took to be a "man" in the ancient world. This scholarship is grounded in theoretical insights about how male and female gender identities have been and are formed. Gender theorists argue that gender identity is not natural. Instead, it is something that is learned and performed. Being masculine or feminine are not biologically given traits. Rather, they are ways of acting in the world. Moreover, studies of masculinities have shown that while there may be different ways to be masculine, often only one form of masculinity is considered the ideal one. This ideal is often reflected in the cultural representations of powerful men.

Using these insights from gender theory, a number of scholars under-took a gender analysis of the rhetoric found in Greek and Roman texts. The results of these studies show agreement on two key points. The first is that writers regularly show concern for proper masculine conduct when they describe public figures. Emperors and other leading men are often praised or blamed on the basis of their manly or "womanish" conduct. Second, these studies show that there is a remarkably consistent set of virtues that are deemed "manly" by these ancient authors.[22]

Most relevant here are the notable overlaps between the virtues at-tributed to Jesus in the Gospel and the virtues associated with being an ideal man in Greco-Roman texts. The writers of those texts agree that dis-playing self-control—over both body and emotions—is the most defining characteristic of a true man. Such self-control was viewed a prerequisite for holding authority over others. Jesus often exhibits this type of control in the Fourth Gospel. Before the Johannine Jesus is arrested and crucified, he makes clear that *he* is the one who is ultimately in control of his life. "No one takes it from me," he claims, "but I lay it down of my own ac-cord. I have power to lay it down, and I have power to take it up again. I have received this command from my Father" (10:18). He claims that the "ruler of this world" (perhaps a reference that encompasses both the Roman emperor and Satan) has no power over him (14:30). Jesus's power and autonomy is on display as he orchestrates events at his own arrest. Note how he steps forward and takes charge of the scene, identifying him-self, striking awe in his captors, and going willingly to his eventual death (18:4-12). When he is supposedly on trial before Pilate, Jesus undercuts the Roman governor's claims of power over him. Any power that Pilate wields is only because God allows him to do so (19:11). Even before dy-ing on the cross, Jesus is shown to be fully in control of the situation as he manages his family affairs, takes care to fulfill scripture, and finally, when he knows that all is finished, gives up his spirit (19:26-30).

Other elements of the Gospel's presentation of Jesus suggest a display of masculinity. We have already noted his intimate relationship to the divine Father as his begotten Son. One could also look to his extended discourses in the Gospel. In the Greco-Roman world, this type of verbal jousting with one's opponents was viewed as a rhetorical display of masculine power.[23] Together, these aspects of the Gospel point to a presentation of Jesus as exemplifying the ideals of the dominant form of masculinity as described in Greco-Roman literature.

But, this is not the whole story. In the same way that not all readers are convinced about the feminine dimension of the Johannine Jesus, so too, not all agree that he measures up to Greco-Roman gender standards of masculinity. For example, Alicia Myers argues that Jesus's displays of masculinity in the Gospel of John are only one part of his gender performance. Another part is his "often off-putting, feminizing behavior."[24] Myers suggests that in the story-world Jesus's opponents perceive him to produce chaos rather than the sort of order that would be produced by rational, manly conduct. Likewise, Jesus's words do not evoke honor from the crowd, but divisiveness. Myer points out that his friends are not among the educated, masculine elite; indeed, his most faithful companions are not even men, but are rather women of diverse backgrounds. Most problematic for a display of manliness is that Jesus's body is penetrated, both with the nails of crucifixion before his death and with a soldier's spear afterward (19:34; 20:20, 25-27). What is more, the evidence of this effeminizing death lingers even after Jesus's resurrection—he maintains the marks of penetration (20:20, 27). This sort of bodily violation undermines claims that the Johannine Jesus displays masculine autonomy and self-control.

Myers explains the Johannine Jesus's masculine *and* feminine conduct by suggesting that he presents a new and redefined masculinity. By reinforcing certain feminine aspects of Jesus's death, the Gospel "refuses to dismiss Jesus' femininity…but retains it as actual femininity that is an integral part of Jesus's identity and mission as God's λόγος" (*logos*).[25] Given the ancient setting of the Gospel, it is not likely that the author had such a view of Jesus in mind. To be convincing one would need to explain *why* this would be a goal in the Gospel's presentation of Jesus. In the midst of a culture that valued men and masculinity much more highly than women and femininity, showing the male hero as also feminine would be quite anachronistic. To be sure, Myers is correct to see that the "ideal" masculinity of Jesus is undermined by the fact of the crucifixion. And, the fact that the author calls attention to the marks of the nails is intriguing. But, if we recall the recognition scene pattern, these marks function as a token, convincing Thomas that the figure before him is one and the same with the Jesus who was crucified. In this way, they are tokens of Jesus's voluntary death, which in this Gospel is defined as his glorification.

Queer Theory and the Gender of the Johannine Jesus

So far, the work I discussed above is focused on two sides of a gender binary: male versus female or masculinity versus femininity. Queer theorists suggest this division is inconsistent with the reality of much lived experience. Like feminist theorists, queer theorists read the biblical text with a goal toward liberation. In this case, this means reading against texts and interpretations that reinforce a man/woman binary, as if the lines between these gender identities are never blurred.

Tat-Siong Benny Liew attempts such a blurring of boundaries in the binary world of the Fourth Gospel in his queer reading of the Johannine Jesus.[26] Note first that Tat-Siong Benny Liew states explicitly that with his queer reading of the Johannine Jesus he is not concerned with authorial intention. The aim of his selective reading and interpretation is "to redress the wrongs that have been suffered by people who have not been gendered strictly as either male or female."[27] In this way, much like feminist theological interpretation intends to provide readings that resist oppressive structures for women, Liew's queer interpretation intends to support people whose gender identity does not fit neatly into the either/ or of a male/female binary. In both cases, the historical question of how an ancient audience might have understood the gendered presentation of Jesus is of less concern than the political aim of bringing justice to an underprivileged group.

Liew begins his interpretation with the debate about the gender of Jesus who is depicted as the incarnate Wisdom of God. As we saw, some scholars see in this a feminine dimension to Jesus, while others argue that any sense of the female personification of Wisdom *Sophia* is erased by the presence of the masculine *logos*. But Liew claims that the real problem of this debate comes from reading the Gospel with an overly rigid view of gender. Looking for either masculine *or* feminine in the character of Jesus, Liew argues, results in "an inability to see and read John's transgendering dynamics."[28]

Liew's interpretation attends to such dynamics. He argues that "there is something quintessentially queer" in the performance of masculinity by the Johannine Jesus. He suggests that Jesus's "beguiling speech" could be tagged as feminine. By this he means the way Jesus uses words with double meanings, or misleads others about his intentions (e.g., John 7:1-10). In addition, the crucifixion depicts the body of Jesus as subject to penetration.[29] But in contrast to Myers, Liew contends that none of this means that Jesus is "really" female, or androgynous, or that he represents a failed masculinity. Instead, it points to the gender complexity of the Johannine Jesus. Rather than arguing for one side or the other of a male/female gender binary, Liew holds up the Gospel as text in which "a range of gender meanings converge, collude, collide, and compete with each other."[30] In doing so, he offers an example of how ideological criticism works. He creatively reads the Gospel in a way that opens it to people who might otherwise feel excluded from the "eternal life" that it offers.

Clearly, these analyses offer widely differing perspectives on how to understand gendered language in the Gospel. Given these divergent interpretations, a student might well wonder which gender analysis is "right." But, this may not be the right question to ask. Scholars who study the nature of language, especially metaphorical language, speak of a "surplus of meaning" that is a part of every literary text. That means that readers can and do find many ways of reading the same text. Interpretations change depending on the context and goals of the interpreter. Thus, feminist interpreters whose goal is to offer gender-inclusive readings of the Gospel for Christian communities in the twenty-first century find resources in the metaphors in the Bible. They may have to read *against* the way this language would have been understood in its ancient, highly androcentric culture.

In contrast, historically oriented gender critics who want to understand precisely what ancient ideas about gender are reflected in the text may have to read against the grain of contemporary feminist interpretations! To be sure, such scholars are also interested in gender inclusivity and justice for women. But, they also understand that uncovering the gender bias in ancient texts are important reminders that ideas about gender *are* culturally constructed and continually in flux. These historically oriented interpretations demonstrate how writings contain deeply embedded ideas about gender that are not in keeping with contemporary values but nevertheless continue to shape the worldviews of readers.

Postcolonial Perspectives on the Gospel of John

In chapter 2, I discussed empire-critical interpretation and the insights this work brings to understanding how the Gospel reflects the reality of negotiating life in the Roman Empire. Postcolonial approaches to the Gospel of John are also interested in the relationship between imperial rule and the narrative, but come at the topic from a different perspective. The starting point for postcolonial analysis is not the Roman Empire *per se*, but more generally the nature of the relationship between the colonizer and the colonized. Postcolonial theorists have studied this relationship at different times and places and noticed common ways that colonizing empires attempt to assert power and control. They have also perceived the different ways colonized peoples negotiate life under foreign domination. Such ways include collaboration with the empire, accommodation to and imitation of the colonizing culture, overt or hidden forms of resistance, or some combination of these responses. Postcolonial critics study literary works that are produced during periods of colonization to discern how they reflect and/or resist imperial ideologies. Postcolonial approaches are ideological because they are concerned about economic, cultural, and social justice in the world. As Muse Dube asserts, "Above all, postcolonialism proposes many different ways to co-exist on earth without having to suppress and exploit the other."[31]

Although postcolonialism originally focused on the effects of late-eighteenth- through mid-twentieth-century European colonialism and decolonization, the phenomenon of imperialism-colonization extends well beyond this particular period in history.[32] Postcolonial critics of the

New Testament argue that insights from postcolonial theory can be fruitfully applied to reading these first-century CE texts.[33]

What does this mean for the Gospel of John? Quite a bit, in fact, because this text is ripe for postcolonial analysis at multiple levels. At one level, one can read the Gospel as a story told about one subgroup of non-Romans negotiating life under Roman occupation. This way of reading overlaps closely with the empire-critical approach. We have already noted how the deliberations by the Jewish council in 11:48 reflect their fear of the Roman occupiers of their land. Later, at the trial of Jesus, "the Jews" evoke Pilate's allegiance to Rome to force his hand against Jesus. "If you release this man, you are no friend of the emperor. Everyone who claims to be a king sets himself against the emperor" (19:12). Then, in an ironic and tragic twist, the Jews under Roman occupation are forced to declare to Pilate, "We have no king but the emperor" (19:15). These examples demonstrate how Rome casts a shadow over all that unfolds in the trial and eventual crucifixion of Jesus.

At another level, a postcolonial interpretation might critique the Gospel's imitation of absolute, cosmic power. In this way, it might differ from many empire-critical interpretations. Postcolonial critics consider the way the Gospel imitates the language of empire in its depiction of God the Father and Jesus as the Son of God and ask, to what effect? Empire-critical readings often emphasize the subversive nature of transferring ruling authority from Rome to God. Postcolonial theorists point to this "mimicry" of empire as a problem of accommodation where the oppressed group uncritically (and unconsciously) adopts the worldview of the oppressor. In the case of the Fourth Gospel, the language of imperial authority is mapped onto an all-powerful deity, in spite of the dangers of adopting this language for God. These dangers become evident once Western Christendom takes on imperial aspirations of its own and the Christian Bible is used to support imperial expansion at the expense of native populations.

Here I offer two examples of postcolonial readings to help clarify this interpretive approach. The first example is from Francisco Segovia, who offers a global reading of the Gospel of John as a postcolonial text that paradoxically adopts "an imperial-like strategy of colonial anti-imperialism."[34]

The second is from Musa Dube who offers a more focused postcolonial of the encounter between Jesus and the Samaritan woman.[35] Note that to fully understand their postcolonial readings, one needs to adopt a reading stance as an outsider. This can be a difficult task since the entire Gospel is written from the perspective of and for the "in-group." Nevertheless, one can adopt a "hermeneutics of otherness and engagement," as Segovia calls it, in order to become more sharply attuned to how the Gospel might fuel imperializing ambitions.

The Gospel as a Postcolonial Text

Segovia's postcolonial reading begins with observations about the Johannine view of reality that is constructed by the Gospel narrative. As we already know, it is a binary, or as he puts it, bipolar world. On one side, there is "this-world" that is "a material world stamped by darkness, death, falsehood, sin." On the other side, there is the "other-world" that is "a spiritual world marked by light, life, truth and grace."[36] But Segovia also notes something curious about the construction of this bipolar world. The narrative never addresses the question of how "this-world" came to be in such an alienated relationship with the "other-world." Why these two realms are so radically opposed to one another and why they are in constant conflict remains an unexplained gap in the narrative. This is especially peculiar since, as we have seen, the narrative also affirms that the world was created by and is loved by God.

Moreover, Segovia argues, the conflict that is reflected in the narrative is cosmic, global, and local in nature. No one is left untouched. He describes this all-encompassing conflict this way: "at a cosmic level between God, sovereign of the world above, and Satan, sovereign of the world below—at the global level, between Jesus, Word of God and savior of the world, and the imperial ruler of Rome—at the local level, between Jesus, Word of God and Messiah of the Jews, and the colonial elite of Judaea."[37] This last group, "the colonial elite," refers to the Jewish leadership in Jerusalem that historically worked collaboratively with Rome to maintain their own local power, especially their authority over the temple.

Segovia points out that the Gospel's "imperial-like strategy" is reflected in its three political tenets: (1) a vertical and hierarchal chain of command between worlds and within worlds that calls for obedience, (2) a rejection of outsiders and condemnation of those who are from "this-world," (3) a rejection of other approaches to the divine and a claim of absolute control over knowledge of God.[38] On this last point, consider the following statements by the Johannine Jesus:

> I am the gate. Whoever enters by me will be saved, and will come in and go out and find pasture. (10:9)

> I am the way, and the truth, and the life. No one comes to the Father except through me. (14:6)

> I have other sheep that do not belong to this fold. I must bring them also, and they will listen to my voice. So there will be one flock, one shepherd. (10:16)

These statements by the Johannine Jesus disallow any legitimate space of coexistence with different groups. Those who have different religious convictions and different modes of being in the world are excluded in favor of the "one flock" with "one shepherd" scenario.

In terms of the Gospel's anti-imperial tendency, Segovia points to the Gospel's vision of the other-world compared to existing visions. The other-world of the Gospel is neither that of Rome, nor of the colonized periphery of Judea. The Roman other-world is home to many different deities, as well as to heroic divinized humans. Indeed, even emperors can make it their home. It is "a divine point of origins or destination for supreme leaders of the political world."[39] The vision of the other-world in the colonial context of Judea allows for the one and only God, surrounded by lower gradations of divine beings. In contrast, the Prologue of the Gospel envisions the other-world as containing one God, "who has engendered an only born god—the Word." This move is radically anti-imperial insofar as this divine authority does not come from the Roman center or even from the colonized periphery. In a world that was filled with constant visual reminders of Roman power, the Gospel presents a God who is known only through the Word. It is not known by way of the Roman Empire, whether through its institutions, practices, or representatives. Nor is this God known by way of the established delegates or representatives of the Jewish nation. In making this move, the Gospel relativizes all claims to power of this-world and in this way, it is radically anti-imperial.

Segovia provides a richly nuanced reading of the plot of John's Gospel as its plot advances on the basis of this paradoxical imperial strategy of anti-imperialism. Of special note is his observation of the way the community that dwells in mutual love clears a space in this-world for the other-world. Segovia likens this space to a colonial outpost in an alien land—an outpost of the kingdom of God in the kingdom of Satan. As a colonial outpost, this space remains complex and thoroughly ambiguous. It stands in complete opposition to this-world, while also replicating the structure and comportment of its imperial target.

Reading for Decolonization

The second more narrowly focused example comes from Musa Dube, who defines herself as "a Motswana woman of Southern Africa." Dube's interpretation of John 4 is done in light of the historical record of using Christian texts to work hand in hand with colonization. Key to her reading is the idea of "imperial travelers" who venture into new territory to expand their power and control. When reading John 4, she envisions Jesus and his disciples moving into the region of Samaria with expansion of their territory in view. Dube's interpretation is detailed and illuminating on many points. Here I can only list some of her main observations about the language and dynamics of the scene at the well in Samaria.

First, Dube notes that John 4 begins with a reference to a competition for power: "the Pharisees had heard 'Jesus is making and baptizing more disciples than John'" (4:1). This reference should be understood in light of the intense competition for power that often occurs with subgroups that are under imperial domination. In this case, Jesus and his disciples, John the Baptist and his disciples, and the Pharisees all vie for allegiance as subgroups under Rome's power. Dube notes that it is this heated competition, which Jesus and his disciples are apparently losing, that spurs Jesus's departure from Judea and their move into Samaria. It is also the reason, Dube suggests, for their turn to proselytizing the Samaritans.

Second, Dube observes how the rhetoric of the story aligns with the idea of imperial expansion. Jesus's observation of fields that are ripe for harvesting suggests the desire to possess and to take what others have worked for (4:35-38). Significantly, these expressions in John 4 recall God's words to Joshua following the conquest of the land of Canaan: "I gave you a land on which you had not labored, and towns that you had not built, and you live in them; you eat the fruit of vineyards and oliveyards that you did not plant" (Josh 24:13). Here, too, Jesus's words take on an air of conquest and capture. The Samaritans are pictured as passive fields waiting, even wanting, to be harvested by the new occupiers. Dube notes that this is typical of imperial ideology that "portrays the colonized as people who 'require and beseech for domination' and the colonizers as people with a moral 'duty to the natives.'"[40] Meanwhile Jesus and his disciples are travelers whose mission is authorized "from above." Their work is both local and global, as the eventual acclamation of Jesus as "savior of the world" reveals. Recall that this was a title reserved for the Roman emperor and directly related to Roman imperial conquest and expansion.

In Dube's interpretation, the Samaritan woman represents her subjugated land. She is portrayed as ignorant, in need of help and morally or religiously lacking something. She does not know what she worships (4:22). Meanwhile, the Johannine Jesus declares that the cultural centers of both Jerusalem (of the Jews) and Gerazim (of the Samaritans) are inadequate. They will be replaced with "true worship" of the Father (4:23-24). In these ways, Dube argues, the ideology of the story is clear: "foreign lands are immoral women which await taming by foreign saviours."[41]

In another essay, Musa Dube and Jeffrey Staley point to the troubling implications of adopting the Gospel's imperial ideology. "Since the [Gospel] narrative prompts the reader/s to identify with the creator, the light and life; to believe and distance themselves from the ignorant who do not believe, it follows that identification with the Word/Jesus could turn readers into possessors of others, possessing the dispossessed and displaced."[42] Thus, in the same way that legacy of Christian anti-Semitism demands serious critique of the Gospel's anti-Jewish rhetoric, so the legacy of Western colonization of the African, South American, and Asian continents demand serious critique of the Gospel's imperializing rhetoric.

There is no doubt that postcolonial interpretations make for troubling reading. For some, the analyses outlined above may be difficult to accept as legitimate interpretations of the Gospel of John. Others may be tempted to reject the text and its colonizing tendencies altogether. But note that neither Segovia nor Dube advocates a rejection of the text. Segovia's project is to bring to light the complex and ambiguous nature of the Gospel's imperial/anti-imperial stance. For her part, Dube urges a reading for "decolonization." Just as feminist critics creatively interpret the text to bring about justice and gender inclusivity, reading for decolonization would creatively read against the text's imperializing rhetoric. As an example, she discusses a rereading of the story of the Samaritan woman in the novel *The Victims* by Mositi Tontontle. In the retelling, the character of a woman dressed in white replaces the character of Jesus. Rather than naming her conversation partner simply "woman" (as the Johannine Jesus does), she calls her "Samaritan woman" several times. In this way, she insists on having the woman maintain her own ethnic identity in their encounter. When the woman in white offers the other woman a drink of "living water," it is from the woman's *own* well. She offers the resources of the woman's own land for sustaining life. Finally, the woman in white sends the Samaritan woman to tell her fellow villagers that "a prophetess has come bringing healing to the broken hearted." Examples like this rereading of John 4 challenge biblical readers to recognize places where one can "acknowledge and embrace" the people and places that have been deemed "heretics and half-breeds." Dube calls for a biblical critical practice that is dedicated to "promoting decolonization, fostering diversity, and imagining liberating ways of interdependence."[43]

Chapter 6

Exploring the Johannine Epistles

Read 1 John, 2 John, and 3 John

In our first read through these texts, I highlighted the many similarities between the Letters and the Gospel, showing why they are considered Johannine literature. When you read them this time, note how these writings differ from the Gospel. Where do you find new ideas, new vocabulary, or different uses of terms that are familiar to you from the Gospel?

More Historical Puzzles: The Who, When, and Why of the Johannine Letters

The Johannine letters hold an important place in the historical study of the Johannine tradition. It is largely because of these three texts that we can even speak of such a tradition or imagine a school or community that produced it. Each of the Letters, written in the first person and addressing a particular audience, seems to give flesh and blood to a group of people who were somehow linked to the Gospel of John. Nevertheless, these letters "tell us virtually nothing about why they were written and who read them."[1] The writer, the audience, and the circumstances for writing are obscured behind the general rhetoric of the Letters. Here is an example of this general way of writing: "They went out from us, but they did not belong to us; for if they had belonged to us, they would have remained with us. But by going out they made it plain that none of them belongs to us" (1 John 2:19).

Here the author clearly signals a departure by a certain "they" and asserts that they didn't belong to "us." Beyond this, he offers no explanation about who this departing group is or why they left. As we know, the author never identifies himself, nor does he indicate when he is writing. Perhaps such details were obvious to the recipients of the letter, but they are no longer obvious to modern interpreters. Scholars are especially interested in determining when the Letters were written in relation to the Gospel. This is because certain details are seen as important clues for reconstructing a history of the Johannine community.

Before discussing how scholars have answered this question of chronology, we should take stock of how the Letters differ from one another and from the Gospel. In terms of the first question, our initial read through the Letters in chapter 1 noted how 2 and 3 John differ from 1 John in writing style. Both 2 and 3 John definitely take the form of personal letters that are sent by someone to someone. In contrast, 1 John is more of a treatise written to a group.

Of the three letters, only 3 John provides insight into a specific situation that is occurring in the church. Among all of the Johannine literature, only 3 John uses the word *ecclesia*, the Greek word for assembly or church. In this letter, the elder praises Gaius who gave hospitality to "friends" of the authors, even though the people were strangers to him. Gaius is then exhorted to send these friends on in a manner worthy of God (3 John 3-6). All of this indicates that Gaius has provided support to traveling missionaries and is now supposed to supply them with provisions for the next stage of their travels. The second part of this brief letter names a certain Diotrephes. In contrast to Gaius, he has refused to comply with prior instructions from the elder to welcome the missionaries. Not only has he refused to do so, but he has also expelled from the church those who did show hospitality to the missionaries (3 John 10). It is unclear whether

Gaius is one of these who has been expelled, or a member of another local church who, unlike Diotrephes, has accepted the authority of the elder.

In contrast to the specificity of 3 John, 2 John reflects the same general language of 1 John. It refers to "many deceivers" who have gone out into the world, and who do not confess that Jesus Christ has come in the flesh (2 John 7). Such a person is an "antichrist." Also in contrast to 3 John, in this letter the elder *prohibits* the letter's recipients from showing hospitality to those outside of the group. "Do not receive into the house or welcome anyone who comes to you and does not bring this teaching," he writes (2 John 10). "This teaching" refers back to the "teaching of Jesus Christ," which could mean either Jesus's own teaching, or the teaching about Jesus Christ.

Given this shared theme of hospitality, some have linked 2 and 3 John sequentially. Perhaps Diotrephes was first refused hospitality by some church members who followed the elder's command. He then responds in kind by refusing and forbidding hospitality, as reflected in 3 John. While this is intriguing speculation, there is not enough evidence in the Letters to make a clear case for such a scenario. What 2 and 3 John do show is that whatever type of group the Johannine community was, they were spread across more than one church. They were within the flow of early traveling missionaries. In this way, the Letters provide evidence of how the Jesus-movement spread in the first and second centuries CE.

First John differs significantly from either 2 or 3 John. As we saw earlier, while they share the style of a personal letter, 1 John is more of a treatise. We also already saw the many overlaps in vocabulary between 1 John and the Gospel, but now you may have noticed how these shared words are not always used in the same way. Here are the two examples from comparing the opening lines of each text:

1) Both writings speak of "the beginning." But the Gospel alludes to the beginning of creation from the Genesis 1 creation account while 1 John declares what was *from* the beginning, referring to the beginning of the revelation of Jesus on earth.

2) Both writings use the term *logos.* The Gospel uses the term on its own, but 1 John uses the term as part of the expression "word of life," a phrase that never appears in the Gospel. In 1 John, it refers to the proclamation about Jesus.

There are other differences between the two writings as well. On the one hand, certain terms one might expect to overlap between the two writings do not. The author of 1 John never uses the word *glory* or *glorification.* The text never refers to the signs of Jesus. Nor does it ever refer to "the Jews." On the other hand, 1 John introduces terms that are not found in the Gospel, such as "antichrist" (2:18, 22; 4:3) or "atoning sacrifice" (2:2; 4:10). Another difference is that 1 John attributes actions to the Father that in the Gospel are attributed to Jesus. For example, in the Gospel, the Johannine Jesus twice issues the command to love one another (13:34; 15:12). In 1 John, the author attributes this command to God (1 John 3:23; see also 2 John 4-5). Some scholars argue that 1 John is more future oriented than the Gospel. The author assures his audience of having "boldness on the day of judgment" (4:17). Similarly, he claims that while the community members are children of God at the present time, what they will become has not yet been revealed (1 John 3:2). Both of these expressions suggest a more traditional Jewish eschatology that envisions God's final judgment at an endpoint in history. As we saw in chapter 4, while the Gospel has some references to this tradition, it more often describes a status that is already present for the believer. These differences are enough for most scholars to conclude that the author of the Letters is not the person who wrote the Gospel. Most interpreters also assume that the "elder" of 2 and 3 John also wrote 1 John, although we cannot even be sure of this. There is no consensus about when the Letters were written in relation to the Gospel. As we will see, scholars read the evidence we just discussed in several different ways.

The Letters and the Gospel: Questions of Chronology

There are many different proposals concerning when the Letters of John were written with respect to the Gospel. Each of these involves the type of analysis that we have just been doing—comparing linguistic data in the Letters (especially 1 John) with the linguistic data in the Gospel. These proposals also involve imagining the historical events that lie behind the writing of the Letters.[2] In what follows, I review three main hypotheses regarding the chronological relationship between the Johannine letters and the Fourth Gospel. These hypotheses include both when the Letters were written vis-à-vis the Gospel and what events lie behind their writing. The discussion that follows relies primarily on evidence from 1 John.

Hypothesis One: The Letters Were Written after the Gospel

This is the majority view among historical critics of the Johannine letters. Scholars who take this position argue that the author of the Letters draws on the metaphorical language and structure of the Gospel. These scholars point especially to similarities between the Gospel's prologue and the opening of 1 John. In this theory, the cluster of similar terms and phrases between these two openings (e.g., beginning, word, life, "was with the Father/God") is seen as evidence that the author of 1 John used the Gospel as inspiration for beginning his own writing.

Those who argue that the Letters came after the Gospel see the Letters reflecting a later stage in the life of the community when it faced a new type of conflict. As we saw in our study of historical approaches to the Gospel of John, many scholars think that the Gospel corresponds to a time when Jewish followers of Jesus were being expelled from a local synagogue community. This situation, they argue, explains the animosity directed toward a group labeled "the Jews" in the Gospel. In contrast, the Letters never use the term "the Jews" to refer to opponents. Thus, the argument goes, they reflect a stage of the community's history that occurred after the separation from the synagogue had already occurred. At this point, the community faced another crisis that was internal to the group of believers. As we saw in chapter 1, evidence for this crisis is linked to the verse we already quoted above. "They went out from us, but they did not belong to us; for if they had belonged to us, they would have remained with us. But by going out they made it plain that none of them belongs to us" (1 John 2:19).

141

Clearly, this verse reflects internal tensions. But what was the dispute about? The author never states this in an explicit way, so many readers look elsewhere in the letter for additional clues about the dispute. This verse has been a prime candidate: "By this you know the Spirit of God: every spirit that confesses that Jesus Christ has come in the flesh is from God, and every spirit that does not confess Jesus is not from God" (1 John 4:2-3).

According to one prominent theory, the deserters left over a christological dispute regarding the humanity of Jesus. This interpretation places the emphasis on the phrase "in the flesh" and reads it as a reference to Jesus's human status. Thus, much like the flesh/glory debate between twentieth-century scholars (see chapter 4 in this book), the community was supposedly arguing about the humanity versus divinity of Jesus. Culpepper's description of the group who left the community reflects this majority position: "Those who had gone out from the community apparently affirmed the divinity of Jesus but denied or diminished the significance of his humanity. The elder insists on the importance of the Incarnation."[3]

Hypothesis Two: The Letters Were Written before the Gospel

Some scholars argue that the Letters reflect an early crisis in the community *before* the Gospel was written. The arguments for this position use the same data as the advocates for the first hypothesis, but interpret it in a different way. For example, scholars who see the Letters as prior to the Gospel note that its opening lines are far less developed than what we see in the poetic grandeur of the Gospel's prologue. They argue that it makes more sense to see the Gospel writer heightening the language from the letter than imaging the process in reverse. For example, *logos* has an elevated cosmic significance in the Gospel, so it would be odd to think that this same term was then reused in 1 John in a more mundane way to refer to preaching. They also note that 1 John's focus on a future end time and its reference to the atoning sacrifice of Jesus are more traditional positions (closer, for example, to ideas expressed in the letters of Paul) than the innovations of the Gospel. Again, one would need to think of a writer reverting back to more traditional positions after the Gospel writer had charted a new path, which some see as unlikely.

One more interesting point in support of the Letters being written before the Gospel concerns the use of the term *paraklētos* in 1 John 2:1. There the author assures the audience that if anyone sins, "we have a *paraklētos* (advocate) with the Father, Jesus Christ the righteous." Apart from the title of "the righteous" for Jesus, which nowhere occurs in the Gospel, Jesus is also named as the *paraklētos*. He is seen as the Advocate who appeals to God on behalf of one who sins. In the Gospel of John, the Advocate is a figure distinct from Jesus. He is "the Holy Spirit" whom Jesus will send after he is gone (14:26; 15:26; 16:7). Most significantly, the Johannine Jesus claims that he will send the disciples "another" advocate (14:16). If the Gospel was written after 1 John, this second advocate would follow the first, who according to the letter, was Jesus.

Scholars who think that 1 John came first view the nature of the intergroup conflict in different ways. Some agree that the group was docetic in its Christology, thinking that Jesus was not actually human. But, they also suggest that part of the point of the Gospel was to present Jesus in a way that refutes this way of thinking. It is offered as a corrective to mistaken ideas about Jesus that were circulating in the community.

Still another minority position does not think the conflict concerns whether Jesus was human but rather whether he was the messiah. Note the following verse that comes soon after the mention of the group who departed at 1 John 2:19: "Who is the liar but the one who denies that Jesus is the Christ? This is the antichrist, the one who denies the Father and the Son" (1 John 2:22). Notice this verse does *not* say, "Who is the one who denies the flesh of Jesus?" Indeed, nothing is mentioned about the flesh or humanity of Jesus, but only his identity as the Christ/messiah. Even the designation "antichrist" suggests this basic idea, rather than the more complex ontological issue of the nature of Jesus's humanity versus divinity. The one who "denies the Father and the Son" would be a denial of the relationship between God and Jesus. Refuting this relationship would not be a denial of the humanity of Jesus, though it might concern

143

the divine status of Jesus. But even more likely, it would be a denial of Jesus as one chosen by God.

And in terms of appealing to 1 John 4:2 to explain the dispute, these scholars suggest that too much weight is put on the phrase "in the flesh." Note that the verse restates the problem as one of "confessing Jesus." There is no repetition of "in the flesh" as one might expect if this was the crucial issue. Given this, the phrase "in the flesh" could simply refer to the fact that Jesus the messiah has actually appeared. No longer must one look forward to the anticipated coming of the messiah. With the coming of Jesus, one could actually see him "in the flesh."

Note that if this hypothesis is correct, those who were going out from the Johannine community may simply have been realigning themselves with the majority view in the synagogue community. In this way, their situation may have resembled the actions of disciples in John 6:66, who "turned back" and no longer went about with Jesus. In any case, the dispute would be very much an inter-Jewish dispute and perhaps still an inter-synagogue dispute. This would be the reason that the phrase "the Jews" does not yet appear in the Letters. The conflict was at an earlier stage where the divisions had not yet hardened between the factions as they had by the time the Gospel was written.

Hypothesis Three: The Letters Should Be Read Independently of the Gospel

A third proposal is that there is simply not enough evidence to determine the relationship between the Letters and the Gospel. Among recent scholars, this has been argued most forcefully by Judith Lieu. Lieu first highlights the problem of circular reasoning that she claims underlies many of the historical reconstructions regarding the relationship between the Johannine letters and Gospel of John. According to Lieu, scholars too often proceed by positing a particular historical reconstruction on the basis of their reading of the text, but then use the text as proof of the correctness of their theory.[4] To give a somewhat silly example of this type of circular reasoning, one might explain the existence of crop circles in the British countryside by positing a history of alien landings on earth.

But one should not then (in a circular way) argue that the crop circles are proof that one's reconstructed history of alien visitation is correct.

In view of this danger of circular reasoning, Judith Lieu has consistently urged Johannine scholars to proceed with caution in their historical reconstruction projects. Her own way of doing this is to read the Letters independently from the Gospel. She argues that there is no need to assume a direct dependence in either direction. One can understand the similarities between these Johannine writings on the basis of a shared Johannine tradition that was deeply familiar to their authors. This assumption of shared knowledge would be in keeping with the idea of a Johannine school, that is, a group of Jesus-followers who shared a common language and vision of the world in relation to God.[5]

At this point, there is no clear consensus on how the Johannine letters relate to the Gospel of John. You may not be surprised to find that there is also no consensus with respect to a literary analysis of the Letters. I turn to this discussion now.

Rhetorical Criticism and the Johannine Epistles

Rather than a literary-critical approach that focuses on narrative elements as was appropriate for the Gospel, the genre of the Letters calls for a different type of literary analysis.[6] In the Greco-Roman world, literary treatises and personal letters had a goal of exhorting the intended audience toward action of some sort. In order to persuade their audience to take a certain course of action, authors drew on conventional patterns of argumentation. This art of persuasion was called rhetoric. The study and practice of ancient rhetoric was necessary for any literate person in the ancient Greco-Roman world.

The way scholars interpret the rhetoric of the Letters corresponds to their theories about the historical circumstances behind the texts. Again, I will focus on the rhetoric of 1 John.

As I mentioned in our initial reading, there is no clear linear structure to the text. Instead, the author interweaves polemical rhetoric about the community's opponents with comforting reassurances to his audience. In doing so, he often circles back to reiterate ideas already stated. Interpreters disagree about how much weight to give to the polemical language compared to the comforting language. Is the main point of 1 John to polemicize against opponents, thereby sharpening the divide between "us" and "them"? Or is it primarily a pastoral letter, written to encourage and strengthen the community?

Those who emphasize the polemical side of 1 John may take the author's many antithetical statements as a reflection of the opposition. So, for example, when the author writes, "If we say that we have no sin" (1 John 1:8), some scholars assume that this is a literal reference to the misguided opponents who are saying they have no sin. Likewise, when the author writes: "Whoever says, 'I have come to know him,' but does not obey his commandments, is a liar, and in such a person the truth does not exist" (1 John 2:4), he is describing the group of deserters. This is certainly possible. On the other hand, the use of antithetical statements was a common feature of ancient rhetoric. It was regularly used to strengthen one's argument by making a parallel contrast, just as the author of 1 John does many times. In short, the rhetoric of 1 John lends itself to multiple interpretations, which I demonstrate through the work of several different scholars below.

John Painter

One way that scholars interpret the combination of polemic and exhortation in 1 John is to imagine that the community is in a severe crisis. John Painter takes this approach. He envisions a community that had suffered emotional pain, confusion, and uncertainty, one that was "traumatized and disturbed" by the departure of the deserters. From his perspective, the comforting language of 1 John is directly related to the break in the community caused by the departure of the opposition group. Thus, Painter argues, "A major aim of 1 John was to rebuild certainty and the joy of a confident faith, all of which had been undermined by the schism."[7]

Pheme Perkins

In contrast to imagining such a major crisis, Pheme Perkins offers an interpretation based on a much different assessment of how the author is using rhetoric. She argues that it is crucial to remember that the writer and his audience lived in what was still primarily an oral culture. This oral culture is reflected, for example, in the similar ways that both 2 and 3 John conclude. The author indicates his preference for a face-to-face conversation rather than using paper and ink (2 John 12; 3 John 13-14). In this oral culture, boys from the upper class were taught from an early age to speak and write in ways that would be persuasive. As Perkins notes, "The point of rhetoric was to use every means possible to see that one's own position, the true or good one, prevailed over its 'bad' opposition."[8] She observes that contemporary readers who are not accustomed to this form of heated debate may overestimate the supposed "crisis" reflected in 1 John. As Perkins puts it, "You would get the impression from reading some modern interpreters of the Johannine letters that the community was being violently ripped apart by the debates to which the author refers."[9] She does acknowledge that a break has occurred and that the writer has in mind an opposing group. But she also suggests that what may sound like an irrevocable break to contemporary readers may be more like a family fight. To her mind, "such disputes do not destroy the whole fabric of a community."[10]

Judith Lieu

Judith Lieu also downplays the idea of a "crisis" as the primary event behind the composition of 1 John. She, too, thinks that scholars have overemphasized the letter's polemical nature.[11] The purpose of 1 John, Lieu argues, is not primarily to engage in debate with or about another group. Instead, she points to what the author says is his purpose at the beginning and end of his work—"the proclamation and assurance of eternal life" (1:2; 5:13; 5:20).[12] Rhetorically, according to Lieu, the letter conveys confidence both about the eternal life that is already known by the community and about how it is known. Note that 1 John uses some form of the verb "to know" thirty-five times across its five chapters. Consider the following assertions:

> Now by this we may be sure that we know him, if we obey his commandments. (1 John 2:3)

> I write to you, not because you do not know the truth, but because you know it, and you know that no lie comes from the truth. (1 John 2:21)

We know that we have passed from death to life because we love one another. Whoever does not love abides in death. (1 John 3:14)

And this final cascade of knowing at the end of the letter:

We know that those who are born of God do not sin, but the one who was born of God protects them, and the evil one does not touch them. **We know** that we are God's children, and that the whole world lies under the power of the evil one. **And we know** that the Son of God has come and has given us understanding so that **we may know** him who is true; and we are in him who is true, in his Son Jesus Christ. He is the true God and eternal life. (1 John 5:18-20, emphasis added)

To be sure, the author does regularly contrast "we" and "you" with another group—"they." But Lieu suggests that this use of pronouns is a rhetorical strategy that creates a sense of fellowship among the group. "They" functions as a contrast to "us" but little more. The opposition group is "defined only by their absence ('going out') and by their act of denial (2:19, 22)." Lieu notes that the author has no interest in the future status of this group. The letter includes no anticipation of their future judgment or condemnation. She suggests that rhetorically and symbolically, "the antichrists embody the specter of failing to remain true: they police the boundaries" between "the world" and the community.[13]

George Parsenios

More recently, in navigating these different interpretations of the rhetoric of 1 John, George Parsenios has taken what he calls a "hybrid" approach. By this Parsenios means that, with Lieu and Perkins, he agrees that the break in the community may not be seen as very serious by the audience to whom 1 John is written. He observes, for example, the apparently ongoing contact with the departing group since the author warns his audience that "they are trying to deceive you" (1 John 3:7). But Parsenios also suggests that the *author* takes the rift very seriously. He argues, "The forceful rhetoric of the letter may not imply that there already is a crisis. Perhaps instead it seeks to produce a crisis."[14] The author writes the letter to make the danger of "pollution by false teaching" clear to the community.

148

In favor of such a hybrid reading is the way the author uses familial terms for his audience such as children and "brothers," coupled with the evocation of the figure of Cain from Genesis 4. If the "brothers" had a dispute, this would certainly be like a family fight. If so, this family fight is certainly intensified when the author claims, "We must not be like Cain who was from the evil one and murdered his brother. And why did he murder him? Because his own deeds were evil and his brother's righteous" (1 John 3:12). This interpretation of the Cain tradition comes in the context of defining the "children of the devil" as those "who do not do right" (1 John 3:10).[15] To follow Parsenios's reading, if the audience perceived of the split as simply a disagreement between "brothers," the author heightens the sense of danger regarding the conflict with this image of fratricide. A few verses later, he offers a further contrast. Far from "murdering" fellow members, the community should lay down their lives for one another (1 John 3:16).

Parsenios's rhetorical analysis goes further by examining the particular rhetorical devices and style adopted by the author. We have already noted the use of antitheses in 1 John. Parsenios notes that the author constructs these antitheses with the use of *sententiae*. This is the Latin designation for brief sayings known as maxims. Maxims communicate some broadly agreed-on truths in a culture. In ancient rhetorical practice, the use of maxims was common. According to Parsenios, their rhetorical purpose was to create boundaries for a community. Those who understood a particular maxim were bound together in their agreement about the truth conveyed in the saying. He highlights the following examples of *sententiae* from the Letters as examples of the broadly agreed-on truths of the community.[16]

God is light and in him there is no darkness at all. (1 John 1:5)

Whoever says, "I am in the light," while hating a brother or sister, is still in the darkness. (1 John 2:9)

And the world and its desire are passing away, but those who do the will of God live forever. (1 John 2:17)

149

For the community, these antithetical maxims set up boundaries between who is in and who is out. Even more, Parsenios argues, these maxims create a world in which one is forced to choose. One cannot sit by as an observer. From the author's perspective, the community has reached a critical point in its existence. In this context, the maxims urge action.

This last point demands further discussion, given the binary structure of the Johannine world. I will return to the issue of choice below. For now, we can say that the evidence from the Letters so far has produced widely varying positions regarding the historical circumstances of their writing and the meaning of their rhetoric. Nevertheless, scholars are more in agreement when it comes to understanding the theological message of these writings. I turn to this discussion now.

Theology and Community in the Johannine Letters

We have already discussed the different christological debates that might lie behind the departure of some people from the community. In this section, I focus on how the assertions about God and Jesus in the Johannine letters connect to a vision of life in the believing community.

In chapter 4 of this book, we saw how the Gospel is focused overwhelmingly on the identity of Jesus—it is Christocentric. The Johannine letters are *theo*centric—the focus is on God. The name *Jesus* is mentioned fourteen times in the Letters. Twelve of these references occur in 1 John. (Notably, 3 John is the only book in the New Testament that never refers to Jesus. That said, at just fifteen verses long, it is also the shortest book in the New Testament.) In some cases, the author of the Letters, like the author of the Gospel, refers to Jesus simply as the Son, or the Son of God. But these are typically in situations where he describes what God has done in relation to his Son (e.g., 1 John 2:22; 3:8; 4:9-10, 14; 5:9-13). Meanwhile, God is mentioned 167 times across the Letters.

First John communicates two major ideas about God. In each case, claims about the nature of God link directly to claims about what this means for life in the community of believers. The first such statement comes at the opening of the body of the letter. Using communal pronouns, the author describes the message that "we" received from Jesus and now proclaim to "you" (plural): "That God is light and in him there is no darkness at all" (1 John 1:5). We are familiar with the symbolism of light from the Gospel where it was used in relation to Jesus, often in contrast to darkness (John 1:4-5, 9; 3:19; 5:35; 8:12). Here it is God who is described as "light" with the implication that "we" must walk in the light rather than darkness (1 John 1:6-7). This "walking in the light" is not defined in detail, but the second major claim provides some indication of what it means to do so.

In 1 John 4, the author twice declares that God is love. In the first instance, this love is defined through God's active sending of the Son:

> Whoever does not love does not know God, for God is love. God's love was revealed among us in this way: God sent his only Son into the world so that we might live through him. In this is love, not that we loved God but that he loved us and sent his Son to be the atoning sacrifice for our sins. Beloved, since God loved us so much, we also ought to love one another. No one has ever seen God; if we love one another, God lives in us, and his love is perfected in us. (1 John 4:8-12)

This passage has strong parallels with the Gospel, but as we should expect, also notable differences. In John 3:16, God so loved the world that he sent his Son. Here, God's love "for us" is revealed in the way he sent his Son into the world. Here the author connects the love of God to sending his Son as an atoning sacrifice, an idea that is not evident in the Gospel. By including this reference, the author makes God's love evident both in the sending of the Son (the incarnation) and in the death of the Son (the crucifixion).[17]

Again, we can find a link between what God is and how the community is to conduct itself. At 1 John 4:19, the author reiterates that God is love, and that "we loved because he first loved us" (1 John 4:19). Both of these references to God loving "us" make clear that love describes not only the nature of God but also the activity of God. Again, this activity is then imitated by the community. "Walking in the light," then, involves loving like God loves. Note, however, that this love is directed only toward others in the community. As in the Gospel, the community is urged to love "one another" (1 John 3:11, 14, 23; 4:7, 11, 12; see John 13:34-35).

151

Several times the author uses the term "perfected" in relation to love (1 John 4:12, 17). The Greek word behind the idea of perfection is *telios*, which means "end" or "completion." Thus, a more helpful translation of the term might be "completed" as in "God lives in us, and his love is completed in us" (1 John 4:12). The idea is not that people love perfectly, but that in loving one another, God's activity of love comes to fruition in and through the community of believers.

Finally, we noted in our first read through of 1 John in chapter 1 the tension in the text around the theme of sin. The tension involves the author's claim that no one who abides in Jesus can sin (1 John 3:4-6). This is not a passing statement as the author goes on to insist: "Those who have been born of God do not sin, because God's seed abides in them; they cannot sin, because they have been born of God" (1 John 3:9). One way to make sense of this claim is to recall that in the Johannine world sin is the same as unbelief. Thus, if one is born from God, one believes, and thus does not sin. Another way, as Judith Lieu suggests, is to see this idea of sinlessness as rooted in the eschatological anticipation of a final age. Where there is a strong sense of this new age already being experienced, as in the Johannine literature, then freedom from sin can already be claimed in the present as well.[18]

This is fine as far as it goes. But, the author also says: "If we say that we have no sin, we deceive ourselves, and the truth is not in us" (1 John 1:8). Perhaps the author is using "sin" in two ways. In the first case, as in the Gospel of John, by definition a believer is unable to sin, precisely because he or she has been born from above and is already participating in the new age. Second, in the more customary sense of sin, even one born of God who "walks in the light," might behave badly on occasion. At such times, one can confess and attain forgiveness (1 John 1:9). This process does not jeopardize one's status as a child of God. Indeed, it is because of this status that one can be "cleansed of all sin." Note that the author appears to sort through these different types of sin in the following verses: "If you see your brother or sister committing what is not a mortal sin, you will ask, and God will give life to such a one—to those whose sin is not mortal.

152

There is sin that is mortal; I do not say that you should pray about that. All wrongdoing is sin, but there is sin that is not mortal" (1 John 5:16-17).

"Mortal sin" is not further defined, but in the Gospel of John, the Johannine Jesus links unbelief to death (John 8:24). Here we might also note the troubling reference to not praying for one who commits a "sin that is mortal." Such an admonition highlights again the highly dualistic nature of the Johannine world, where outsiders are seemingly forever on the outside. This leads to our final section on ideological criticism.

Ideological Criticism and the Johannine Letters

Given the Letters' brevity, scholars have not engaged in extensive ideological criticism of the Johannine epistles. But, there are certain elements that could fruitfully be explored. From a gender-critical perspective, it is notable that these letters do not name any women (unlike the letters of Paul). The "elder" who writes is a male figure, as are the only other named individuals—Gaius and Diotrephes. The designations used by the community are either male (brothers) or gender neutral (children, beloved). At one point, the author specifies that he is writing to fathers, to young men, and to children (1 John 2:12-14). These primarily male designations are not surprising given the way language commonly reflects patriarchal culture in designations for groups of people (consider "mankind," which persists in the English language, despite the available gender-neutral alternative "humankind"). Nevertheless, the strongly masculine designations for the addressees is curious given the presence of so many individual female characters in the Gospel.[19] It certainly raises questions about the arguments for women leadership in the Johannine community.

To be sure, there is one major reference to a female figure in the salutation of 2 John. As we have seen, the elder writes to the elect "lady" in verse 1 (Gk. *kyria*, see also 2 John 5). A corresponding phrase comes at the close of the letter, where the elder passes on greetings from "the children of your elect sister" (2 John 13). Taken together, "lady" is clearly a designation for local churches. Personifying the community of believers as female, especially as a bride to Christ, is common across New Testament writings and follows a long tradition of personifying the people of Israel as a woman in relation to God.[20]

Another interesting detail related to our earlier gender analysis of the Fourth Gospel is the author's repeated use of "begotten" (*gennaō*) to refer to those born of God (e.g., 2:29; 3:1; 5:1, 4, 18). As in the Gospel of John, this term refers to the masculine side of procreation. Much like the Son was begotten of the Father, so too, the author envisions the "children" to whom he writes as being "fathered" by God, with the role of the mother nowhere in view.

In terms of a post-colonial analysis one could easily raise the same sort of questions that one asks of the Gospel. In particular, one might center on the binary construction of human existence as "us" versus "them" and the stark lines drawn between the two. Indeed, from a post-colonial perspective the rhetorical force of the Letters reinforces the sort of border formation—defining who is in and who is out, who is "native" and who is "civilized"—that is a common characteristic of colonizing literature.

In fact, what I did not mention earlier in the discussion of Parsenios's analysis of the Johannine maxims is that his argument draws on an article titled "The Pleasures of Imperialism" by the prominent postcolonial theorist Edward Said (pronounced *sah-eed*). Parsenios uses the insights of Said to describe the border-forming function of maxims in 1 John. It is worth exploring Said's argument a bit further to understand its implications for reading 1 John. In his essay, Said is discussing a novel titled *Kim* by Rudyard Kipling. We already noted the work of Kipling in Dube's postcolonial analysis of John. Here we can look to Said's analysis of *Kim* to notice more about 1 John. Said notes the many editorial asides scattered throughout the novel that define "the immutable nature of the Oriental world as distinguished from the white world, no less immutable." Such asides include comments like "Kim was lying like an Oriental." "Being natives" explains why a group of men did not work to unload a truck. Similarly, "The Oriental's indifference to mere noise" is offered as the reason why the novel's protagonist can sleep on a noisy train.[21] Said's point is that such expressions of "conventional wisdom" are simply ideas derived from British perceptions of India. When offered as objective truths, they solidify these perceptions as reality.

Something similar occurs in 1 John. Two opposing sides are drawn, defined, and presented as immutable. Perkins notes the problem when she writes: "This emphasis on the static quality of what the believer 'is' and its dualist setting, particularly in 3:7-10, begins to suggest two divinely intended groups fixed in an unchanging opposition which has been mysteriously generated by the polarity in the divine world between God and the devil."[22]

Both Lieu and Parsenios suggest that what is different about the dualistic world of the Johannine letters is that one can make a choice. Believing and loving one's brother are acts of the will.[23] Thereby, the problematic nature of these antithetical maxims is resolved. I suggest that as with the characters in the Johannine Gospel narrative, so also with the binary world of 1 John, there is little indication of choice, but rather the revealing of what one actually is (child of God or child of the devil). There is no effort of persuasion directed toward the outsiders—they are outside now and seemingly forever. The Johannine literature, for all its beauty, is a group of writings that works hard to solidify and defend the borders of the world it constructs.

In contrast, there is a growing body of research on the first three centuries CE that suggests that the daily interchange between Jews, Gentiles, and emerging Christian communities was far more porous than might be assumed from certain writings from the period. Note that in 2 John, for example, the very prohibition against hospitality to those outside of the elder's teaching implies that it may well have been taking place. In short, perhaps the divisions were not experienced in the community as sharply as the author of the Letters may have wished.

In light of this, we might read between the lines of the Johannine literature and probe its general hostility toward "otherness." Certainly, there are some theological ideas that need to be rejected from a Christian perspective. But in the case of the Letters of John, we cannot even be sure what those ideas are! All we know is that "they" do not belong to "us." On this point, we might consider again the proposal of postcolonialism that "there are many different ways to co-exist on earth without having to suppress and exploit the other."[24] Perhaps one such way is to extend the Johannine command to love one another to include the idea of love of the "other."

Notes

1. Getting to Know the Johannine Literature

1. A slightly modified version of a statement by Wayne Meeks in Wayne A. Meeks, "The Man from Heaven in Johannine Sectarianism," *Journal of Biblical Literature* 91 (1972): 68. The original quotation reads, "The reader cannot understand any part of the Fourth Gospel until he understands the whole."

2. George L. Parsenios, *First, Second, and Third John* (Grand Rapids: Baker Academic, 2014), 9. For a full list of common vocabulary and phrases see the detailed charts in ibid., 6–8.

2. Exploring Historical Puzzles in the Gospel of John

1. The ancient manuscripts differ in the verb form. Some have a present subjunctive, "that you continue to believe," while some have an aorist subjunctive "that you may come to believe."

2. It is often easier for students of the Gospel to understand this sort of development of Jesus traditions after reading the Infancy Gospel of Thomas. This second-century gospel fills in the "untold story" about Jesus's boyhood in ways that both amuse and surprise contemporary readers. The gospel depicts a boy-Jesus who has not yet learned to wield his miraculous superpowers appropriately, and so, for example, strikes dead a boy who has accidently bumped into him. See http://www.early christianwritings.com/text/infancythomas-hock.html.

3. Readers interested in questions of the historical accuracy of the Johannine traditions should consult the three volumes published by the "John, Jesus and History" group that convened annually from 2002 to 2016 at the Society of Biblical Literature. See Paul N. Anderson, Felix Just, and Tom Thatcher, eds., *John, Jesus, and History*, Society of Biblical Literature Symposium Series (Atlanta, GA: Society of Biblical Literature, 2007). A recent trend in historical Jesus studies concerns the use of social memory theory. For application of this theory in relation to the Gospel of John, see Tom Thatcher, *Why John Wrote a Gospel: Jesus—Memory—History*, 1st ed. (Louisville, KY: Westminster John Knox Press, 2006).

4. Current proposals range from the late first century through the third century CE, making it a moving target for dating the Gospel of John. For a call for reassessment of the use of P 52 see Brent Nongbri, "The Use and Abuse of P52: Papyrological Pitfalls in the Dating of the Fourth Gospel," *Harvard Theological Review* 98 (2005).

5. Scholars differ in assessing whether Origen and Ignatius allude to the Gospel. For a more positive assessment see Charles E. Hill, *The Johannine Corpus in the Early Church* (Oxford; New York: Oxford University Press, 2004).

6. In a disturbing coincidence, on the same day that I was finishing up the final revisions for this book, I heard a news account playing in the background about a white supremacist group that was chanting anti-Semitic slogans and carrying signs claiming that Jewish people are "children of Satan." Clearly, some of the rhetoric that is present in the Gospel is still being used for nefarious ends.

7. J. Louis Martyn, *History and Theology in the Fourth Gospel*, 3rd ed. (Louisville, KY: Westminster John Knox Press, 2003), 16.

8. Ibid.

9. Bultmann and others posited a pre-Christian Gnostic background to the Gospel because they were not aware of parallels within Second Temple Judaism to the type of ideas expressed in the Gospel of John. The discovery of the Dead Sea Scrolls, however, showed that certain

forms of ancient Judaism also contained a strongly dualistic worldview, much like the Johannine literature. For a review of the impact of the scrolls on Johannine research see Mary L. Coloe and Tom Thatcher, eds., *John, Qumran, and the Dead Sea Scrolls: Sixty Years of Discovery and Debate* (Atlanta: Society of Biblical Literature, 2011).

10. Some have seen this more as a "school" along the lines of other ancient schools, or a "circle" but the designation "community" has stuck. See R. Alan Culpepper, *The Johannine School: An Evaluation of the Johannine-School Hypothesis Based on an Investigation of the Nature of Ancient Schools* (Missoula, MT: Scholars Press for the Society of Biblical Literature, 1975); Oscar Cullmann, *The Johannine Circle: Its Place in Judaism, among the Disciples of Jesus and in Early Christianity: A Study in the Origin of the Gospel of John* (London: S.C.M. Press, 1976); Udo Schnelle, *Antidocetic Christology in the Gospel of John: An Investigation of the Place of the Fourth Gospel in the Johannine School* (Minneapolis: Fortress Press, 1992).

11. Raymond E. Brown, *The Community of the Beloved Disciple* (New York: Paulist Press, 1979). Brown acknowledges the speculative nature of his work when he claims he will be happy if his readers accept even 60 percent of his "detective work" (7).

12. The church writer John Chrysostom's strong admonitions for his readers to shun the synagogue in his *Against the Jews* only makes sense in a context where Christians living in Antioch were still taking part in Jewish festivals.

13. Seth Schwartz, *Imperialism and Jewish Society, 200 B.C.E. to 640 C.E.* (Princeton, NJ: Princeton University Press, 2001).

14. Richard Bauckham, *The Gospels for All Christians: Rethinking the Gospel Audiences* (Grand Rapids: Wm. B. Eerdmans, 1998).

15. Adele Reinhartz, "The Johannine Community and Its Jewish Neighbors: A Reappraisal," in *What Is John? Vol. 2, Literary and Social Readings of the Fourth Gospel*, ed. Fernando F. Segovia (Atlanta: Scholars Press, 1998).

16. Meeks, "The Man from Heaven in Johannine Sectarianism." Meeks did not agree, however, with Martyn's proposal to link the expulsion to the *Birkat ha-Minim*. See p. 55n50.

17. Brown argued against the designation, asserting that author did not see the group as separate from other Jesus-followers (see Brown, *The Community of the Beloved Disciple,* 88–91). Nevertheless, a consistent line of scholarship continues to posit and analyze the sectarian nature of the Johannine community. For a more recent discussion see Carsten Claussen, "John, Qumran, and the Question of Sectarianism," *Perspectives in Religious Studies* 37 (2010). Jerome Neyrey has also made extensive use of social science categories for interpretation of the Gospel, especially by applying concepts from cultural anthropology to the ancient Mediterranean context of the Gospel. See Jerome H. Neyrey, *The Gospel of John in Cultural and Rhetorical Perspective* (Grand Rapids: Wm. B. Eerdmans, 2009).

18. Raimo Hakola, *Reconsidering Johannine Christianity: A Social Identity Approach* (New York: Routledge, Taylor & Francis Group, 2015).

19. Warren Carter, *John and Empire: Initial Explorations* (New York: T & T Clark, 2008). Other empire-critical studies of the Gospel include Tom Thatcher, *Greater Than Caesar: Christology and Empire in the Fourth Gospel* (Minneapolis: Fortress Press, 2009).

20. Carter is not necessarily assuming the Gospel was written in Ephesus, but he does reasonably assume that Jesus-believers living in Ephesus would have read the Gospel.

21. See Paul Zanker, *The Power of Images in the Age of Augustus* (Ann Arbor: University of Michigan Press, 1990). Carter lists nine different means of control exerted by Roman authorities: small bureaucracy whose primary function was to collect taxes, alliances with local elites, economic control, taxes and tributes, military power, patron-client relations, imperial theology, rhetoric and justice. Carter, *John and Empire: Initial Explorations,* 55–58.

22. See also Thatcher, *Greater Than Caesar: Christology and Empire in the Fourth Gospel.*

23. Carter, *John and Empire: Initial Explorations,* 227.

3. Exploring Literary Design in the Gospel of John

1. R. Alan Culpepper, *Anatomy of the Fourth Gospel: A Study in Literary Design* (Philadelphia: Fortress Press, 1983), 5. For an anthology of literary readings of the Gospel see Mark W. G. Stibbe, *The Gospel of John as Literature: An Anthology of Twentieth-Century Perspectives* (Leiden; New York: E.J. Brill, 1993).

2. Richard A. Burridge, *What Are the Gospels? A Comparison with Graeco-Roman Biography* (Grand Rapids: Eerdmans, 2004).

3. See the discussion in Kasper Bro Larsen, ed., *The Gospel of John as Genre Mosaic* (Göttingen; Bristol, CT: Vandenhoeck & Ruprecht, 2015).

4. Adele Reinhartz, *The Word in the World: The Cosmological Tale in the Fourth Gospel* (Atlanta: Scholars Press, 1992), 16.

5. Ibid., 18–25. Reinhartz also identifies an "ecclesiological tale," which is the story of the community behind the Gospel.

6. Kasper Bro Larsen, *Recognizing the Stranger: Recognition Scenes in the Gospel of John* (Leiden; Boston: Brill, 2008), 5.

7. Mark Stibbe refers to these aspects as the Gospel's main plot ("Jesus' quest to the work of his Father") and a counterplot ("the Jews drive to destroy Jesus"). Mark W. G. Stibbe, *John as Storyteller: Narrative Criticism and the Fourth Gospel* (Cambridge; New York: Cambridge University Press, 1992).

8. I discuss the Johannine Jesus as God's agent in chapter 4.

9. Although Brown did not read as a literary critic, he famously identified this point as the shift from the "book of signs" (chapters 1–12), to the "book of glory" (chapters 13–21). As Francisco Segovia rightly points out, before the advent of literary criticism of the Gospel, a concern with understanding the overall "structure" of the Gospel already revealed a sensitivity to what we are here calling the plot. Fernando F. Segovia, "The Journey(s) of the Word of God: A Reading of the Plot of the Fourth Gospel," *Semeia* 53 (1991): 26–28.

10. Fernando Segovia's proposal for understanding the plot of the Gospel is based on this journey motif, another common convention in ancient biographies. Ibid.

11. See Larsen, *Recognizing the Stranger: Recognition Scenes in the Gospel of John*, 63–71. In discussing these elements of ancient recognition scenes, Larsen makes clear that not all these moves are always present in this same order and also demonstrates the variety of ways such scenes can unfold.

12. See especially Stibbe, *John as Storyteller: Narrative Criticism and the Fourth Gospel.*

13. Larsen, *Recognizing the Stranger: Recognition Scenes in the Gospel of John.* Larsen notes that no one ever addresses Jesus with his proper name in the Gospel.

14. Culpepper, *Anatomy of the Fourth Gospel: A Study in Literary Design*, 105.

15. The apple analogy comes from Adele Berlin, *Poetics and Interpretation of Biblical Narrative* (Sheffield: Almond Press, 1983), 13–14.

16. Jo-Ann A. Brant, *Dialogue and Drama: Elements of Greek Tragedy in the Fourth Gospel* (Peabody, MA: Hendrickson Publishers, 2004), 57.

17. Ibid.

18. In this section on character and recognition scenes, I draw on the fine analysis of Kasper Bro Larsen. Larsen, *Recognizing the Stranger: Recognition Scenes in the Gospel of John.*

19. The story is a good example of the "genre mosaic" of the Gospel. Many readers have interpreted the story as a play on the Jewish betrothal scenes in the Hebrew Bible, where the patriarch meets his future wife at a well. Larsen shows how the scene also, and perhaps more closely, parallels the Greek recognition type scene.

20. Larsen, *Recognizing the Stranger: Recognition Scenes in the Gospel of John*, 133.

21. Ibid., 223.

22. This is how the famous church writer Augustine of Hippo understood the passage.

23. Brant, *Dialogue and Drama: Elements of Greek Tragedy in the Fourth Gospel*, 184–85.

24. George L. Parsenios, *Departure and Consolation: The Johannine Farewell Discourses in Light of Greco-Roman Literature* (Leiden; Boston: Brill, 2005).

25. Brant, *Dialogue and Drama: Elements of Greek Tragedy in the Fourth Gospel*, 187.

26. Culpepper, *Anatomy of the Fourth Gospel: A Study in Literary Design*, 151.

4. Exploring the Theology of the Gospel of John

1. The Council of Nicaea in 325 CE debated the question of the nature of Jesus, declaring that the Son was of the same substance as God the Father. The Council of Chalcedon in 451 CE continued to refine this position, stating that Jesus was of two natures—fully God and fully human.

2. For a review of scholarship on research into Johannine Christology see Paul N. Anderson, *The Christology of the Fourth Gospel: Its Unity and Disunity in the Light of John 6* (Tübingen: Mohr, 1996).

3. As we saw in the last chapter, perhaps the most relevant example for the Gospel of John is the god Dionysus as depicted in Euripides's *The Bacchae*.

4. Rudolf Bultmann, *The Gospel of John: A Commentary* (Philadelphia: Westminster Press, 1971), 63.

5. Ibid., 63.

6. Ernst Käsemann, *The Testament of Jesus: A Study of the Gospel of John in the Light of Chapter 17* (London: S.C.M. Press, 1968), 9.

7. Ibid., 75.

8. For example see John F. O'Grady, "The Human Jesus in the Fourth Gospel," *Biblical Theology Bulletin* 14 (1984); Jerome H. Neyrey, "'My Lord and My God': The Divinity of Jesus in John's Gospel," *Society of Biblical Literature Seminar Papers* 25 (1986); Marianne Meye Thompson, *The Humanity of Jesus in the Fourth Gospel* (Philadelphia: Fortress Press, 1988). Paul Anderson suggests that the dialectical tension between flesh and glory should be maintained. For him, it represents the complexity of thought of the evangelist. Anderson, *The Christology of the Fourth Gospel: Its Unity and Disunity in the Light of John 6.*

9. See chapter 2, pages 44–45 for discussion.

10. Neyrey, "'My Lord and My God': The Divinity of Jesus in John's Gospel," 163. Neyrey is here agreeing with Meeks's analysis.

11. For example see Gunther Bornkamm, "Towards the Interpretation of the Fourth Gospel: A Discussion of *The Testament of Jesus* by Ernst Kasemann," in *The Interpretation of John*, ed. John Ashton (Philadelphia; London: Fortress Press; SPCK, 1986).

12. See the entertaining discussion of these human-like gods in Giulia Sissa, *The Daily Life of the Greek Gods* (Stanford, CA: Stanford University Press, 2000).

13. See for example the work of Dorothy A. Lee, *Flesh and Glory: Symbol, Gender, and Theology in the Gospel of John* (New York: Crossroad, 2002).

14. For more on textual criticism see Kurt Aland and Barbara Aland, *The Text of The New Testament: An Introduction to the Critical Editions and to the Theory and Practice of Modern Textual Criticism* (Grand Rapids: Wm. B. Eerdmans, 1989); Bruce M. Metzger, *The Text of the New Testament: Its Transmission, Corruption, and Restoration*, ed. Bart D. Ehrman (New York: Oxford University Press, 2005).

15. Sharon H. Ringe, *Wisdom's Friends: Community and Christology in the Fourth Gospel* (Louisville, KY: Westminster John Knox Press, 1999), 29.

16. For more extensive discussion see Raymond E. Brown, *The Gospel According to John (I–Xii)*, The Anchor Bible (Garden City, NY: Doubleday, 1966), cxxii–cxxv; Martin Scott, *Sophia and the Johannine Jesus* (Sheffield: Sheffield Academic Press, 1992); Ringe, *Wisdom's Friends: Community and Christology in the Fourth Gospel.*

17. Beth M. Stovell, *Mapping Metaphorical Discourse in the Fourth Gospel: John's Eternal King* (Leiden; Boston: Brill, 2012).

18. Ibid., 300.

19. Warren Carter, *Pontius Pilate: Portraits of a Roman Governor* (Collegeville, MN: Liturgical Press, 2003), 136.

20. Mary L. Coloe, *God Dwells with Us: Temple Symbolism in the Fourth Gospel* (Collegeville, MN: Liturgical Press, 2001), 214. See also Stephen T. Um, *The Theme of Temple Christology in John's Gospel* (London; New York: T & T Clark, 2006). Um focuses on the temple imagery of water and spirit in John 4.

21. Coloe, *God Dwells with Us: Temple Symbolism in the Fourth Gospel*, 167.

22. Peder Borgen, "God's Agent in the Fourth Gospel," in *Religions in Antiquity: Essays in Memory of Erwin Ramsdell Goodenough*, ed. Jacob Neusner (Leiden: E. J. Brill, 1968).

23. Ibid., 140.

24. William R. G. Loader, "Central Structure of Johannine Christology," *New Testament Studies* 30 (1984): 77. See now the more extended discussion in William Loader, *Jesus in John's Gospel: Structure and Issues in Johannine Christology* (Grand Rapids: Wm. B. Eerdmans, 2017), 41–146.

25. I use the masculine pronoun for God because the Gospel of John depicts God in masculine terms. I discuss the implications of this gendered language for God in the next chapter.

26. For discussion of the presentation of God in John 5:1-30 see Warren Carter, *God in the New Testament* (Nashville: Abingdon Press, 2016), 81–92.

5. Exploring Ideology in the Gospel of John

1. Sandra M. Schneiders, "Women in the Fourth Gospel and the Role of Women in the Contemporary Church," *Biblical Theology Bulletin* 12 (1982): 40. Schneiders makes clear that her interpretation of the Gospel is motivated by a desire to balance years of male-dominated exegesis. Notably, the first sustained discussion of women in the Gospel was done by a Roman Catholic priest and biblical scholar. See Raymond E. Brown, "Roles of Women in the Fourth Gospel," *Theological Studies* 36 (1975). Republished as an appendix to *The Community of the Beloved Disciple*. Brown concludes that "this seems to have been a community where in the things that really mattered in the following of Christ there was no difference between male and female" (693). Nevertheless, he grants only "quasi-apostolic" roles to the Samaritan woman and Mary Magdalene.

2. For a review of twentieth-century "roles of women" scholarship see Colleen M. Conway, *Men and Women in the Fourth Gospel: Gender and Johannine Characterization* (Atlanta: Society of Biblical Literature, 1999), 18–36.

3. For more extended discussion see my "Gender Matters in John," in *A Feminist Companion to John*, ed. Amy-Jill Levine (Cleveland: Pilgrim, 2003).

4. Lee, *Flesh and Glory: Symbol, Gender, and Theology in the Gospel of John*, 5.

5. Scott, *Sophia and the Johannine Jesus*, 244. Scott also explains the presence of the female characters on the basis of wisdom Christology—they

function as "handmaids to Sophia" (for reference to these handmaids see Prov 9:3).

6. Ibid., 172.

7. J. Massyngberde Ford, *Redeemer—Friend and Mother: Salvation in Antiquity and in the Gospel of John* (Minneapolis: Fortress Press, 1997).

8. Lee, *Flesh and Glory: Symbol, Gender, and Theology in the Gospel of John*, 140. Lee is referring to the depiction of Isis in the Latin writer Apuleius's *Metamorphoses*.

9. Meeks, "The Man from Heaven in Johannine Sectarianism," 72.

10. Elisabeth Schüssler Fiorenza, *Jesus: Miriam's Child, Sophia's Prophet: Critical Issues in Feminist Christology* (New York: Continuum, 1994), 153.

11. Judith Lieu, "Scripture and the Feminine in John," in *A Feminist Companion to the Hebrew Bible in the New Testament*, ed. Athalya Brenner (Sheffield, England: Sheffield Academic Press, 1996), 299. For additional discussion of the use of wisdom and gender in the Gospel see Colleen M. Conway, "'Behold the Man!' Masculine Christology and the Fourth Gospel," in *New Testament Masculinities*, ed. Stephen D. Moore and Janice Capel Anderson (Atlanta: Society of Biblical Literature, 2003), 175–79.

12. Gail R. O'Day, "Gospel of John," in *Women's Bible Commentary*, ed. Carol A. Newsom, Sharon H. Ringe, and Jacqueline E. Lapsley (Louisville, KY: Westminster John Knox, 2014), 530.

13. Lee, *Flesh and Glory: Symbol, Gender, and Theology in the Gospel of John*, 126.

14. Ibid., 124.

15. Ibid., 155.

16. Ibid., 159.

17. Overlapping Greek terms include *arche* (beginning), *logos*, (not "word" but the male generative seed in Aristotle's use), *monogenes* (only begotten), and forms of the verb *ginomai* (to become).

18. The theory is detailed Aristotle's treatise titled *On the Generation of Animals.*

19. Turid Karlsen Seim, "Descent and Divine Paternity in the Gospel of John: Does the Mother Matter?," *New Testament Studies* 51 (2005): 364. See also "Motherhood and the Making of Fathers in Antiquity: Contextualizing Genetics in the Gospel of John," in *Women and Gender in Ancient Religions: Interdisciplinary Approaches,* ed. Paul A. Holloway, Stephen P. Ahearne-Kroll, and James A. Kelhoffer (Tübingen: Mohr Siebeck, 2010).

20. Seim, "Descent and Divine Paternity in the Gospel of John: Does the Mother Matter?," 373.

21. Ibid., 375.

22. See Maud W. Gleason, *Making Men: Sophists and Self-Presentation in Ancient Rome* (Princeton, NJ: Princeton University Press, 1995); Lin Foxhall and J. B. Salmon, *When Men Were Men: Masculinity, Power, and Identity in Classical Antiquity* (London; New York: Routledge, 1998); *Thinking Men: Masculinity and Its Self-Representation in the Classical Tradition* (London; New York: Routledge, 1998); Craig A. Williams, *Roman Homosexuality: Ideologies of Masculinity in Classical Antiquity* (Oxford; New York: Oxford University Press, 1999, rev. ed., 2010).

23. I discuss the masculinity of Jesus in more detail in Colleen M. Conway, *Behold the Man: Jesus and Greco-Roman Masculinity* (Oxford; New York: Oxford University Press, 2008); Conway, "'Behold the Man!' Masculine Christology and the Fourth Gospel."

24. Alicia D. Myers, "Gender, Rhetoric and Recognition: Characterizing Jesus and (Re)Defining Masculinity in the Gospel of John," *Journal for the Study of the New Testament* 38 (2015): 207.

25. Ibid., 212.

26. Tat-siong Benny Liew, "Queering Closets and Perverting Desires: Cross-Examining John's Engendering and Transgendering Word across Different Worlds," in *They Were All Together in One Place? Toward Minority Biblical Criticism*, ed. Randall C. Bailey, Tat-siong Benny Liew, and Fernando F. Segovia (Leiden; Boston: Brill, 2009).

27. Ibid., 261.

28. Ibid.

29. Ibid., 266.

30. Ibid., 260.

31. Musa W. Dube and Jeffrey L. Staley, "Descending from and Ascending into Heaven: A Postcolonial Analysis of Travel, Space and Power in John," in *John and Postcolonialism: Travel, Space and Power*, ed. Musa W. Dube and Jeffrey L. Staley (London; New York: Sheffield, 2002), 3.

32. For an introduction to postcolonial theory see Leela Gandhi, "Postcolonial Theory: A Critical Introduction" (New York: Columbia University Press, 1998); Jane Hiddleston, "Understanding Postcolonialism" (Stocksfield: Acumen, 2009).

33. For a discussion of postcolonialism in relation to the biblical interpretation see Stephen D. Moore, "Postcolonialism," in *Handbook of Postmodern Biblical Interpretation*, ed. A. K. M. Adam (St. Louis, MO: Chalice Press, 2000); *Empire and Apocalpyse: Postcolonialism and the New Testament* (Sheffield: Sheffield Phoenix Press, 2006); R. S. Sugirtharajah, ed., *The Postcolonial Biblical Reader* (Malden, MA: Blackwell, 2006).

34. Fernando F. Segovia, "The Gospel of John," in *A Postcolonial Commentary on the New Testament Writings*, ed. Fernando F. Segovia and R. S. Sugirtharajah (London: T & T Clark, 2009), 192.

35. Musa W. Dube, "Reading for Decolonization (John 4:1-42)," in *John and Postcolonialism: Travel, Space and Power* (London; New York: Sheffield, 2002).

36. Segovia, "The Gospel of John," 166.

37. Ibid., 168.

38. Ibid., 169.

39. Ibid.

40. The quoted lines are references to the rationalization made by Europeans for their colonizing efforts. Dube points, for example, to Rudyard Kipling's 1899 poem called "The White Man's Burden," which legitimates European colonization by way of Christian mission. See Dube, "Reading for Decolonization (John 4:1-42)," 65 and 60n37.

41. Ibid., 71.

42. Musa W. Dube and Jeffrey L. Staley, "Descending from and Ascending into Heaven: A Postcolonial Analysis of Travel, Space and Power in John," ibid., ed. Musa W. Dube and Jeffrey L. Staley, 10.

43. Musa W. Dube, "Reading for Decolonization (John 4:1-42)," ibid., 75.

6. Exploring the Johannine Epistles

1. Parsenios, *First, Second, and Third John*, 3.

2. For a comprehensive review of various proposals see "The Relationship Between the Gospel and 1 John," in *Communities in Dispute: Current Scholarship on the Johannine Epistles*, ed. R. Alan Culpepper and Paul N. Anderson (Atlanta: SBL Press, 2014).

3. R. Alan. Culpepper, *The Gospel and Letters of John*, Interpreting Biblical Texts Series (Nashville: Abingdon Press, 1998), 268.

4. Judith M. Lieu, "The Audience of the Johannine Epistles," in *Communities in Dispute: Current Scholarship on the Johannine Epistles*, ed. R. Alan Culpepper and Paul N. Anderson (Atlanta: SBL Press, 2014), 123–24.

5. Yet another proposal is that letters were written at some contemporaneous point to the composition of the Gospel. Scholars following this theory posit that an editor of a later stage of the Gospel also wrote the Letters. In this view, whoever expanded the Gospel may also have written the Letters. But these discussions involve complex theories of the Gospel's composition in relation to 1 John that go beyond this introduction to the Gospel and Letters.

6. However Lieu does explore the narrative "embodied" by the Letters. She argues that ancient letters contain a narrative insofar as they reflect past events, anticipate future ones, and themselves play a role in linking past and present. See Lieu, "The Audience of the Johannine Epistles," 132–35.

7. John Painter and Daniel J. Harrington, *1, 2, and 3 John* (Collegeville, MN: Liturgical Press, 2002), 78.

8. Pheme Perkins, *The Johannine Epistles* (Wilmington, DE: Michael Glazier, 1979), xxii.

9. Ibid., xxi.

10. Ibid., xxii–xxiii.

11. Judith Lieu, *The Theology of the Johannine Epistles* (Cambridge; New York: Cambridge University Press, 1991), 15–16.

12. Ibid., 22.

13. Lieu, "The Audience of the Johannine Epistles," 137.

14. Parsenios, *First, Second, and Third John*, 16.

15. Note that this author's explanation for Cain's murder of Abel is an interpretation that is not supported by the Genesis account. There is no indication of Cain "doing evil" before the murder of his brother Abel.

16. Parsenios, *First, Second, and Third John*, 17.

17. Once again, I am following the language of the text in using gender-specific language. The author draws on the same Father/Son imagery

that the author of the Gospel does. Ideally, especially for liturgical uses, one might translate, "God's sent God's son..."

18. Lieu, *The Theology of the Johannine Epistles*, 58–59.

19. Note that the NRSV translation includes "sisters" in its translation at 1 John 3:10, 13; 4:20-21. The word for "sisters" is not present in the Greek text, but the translators are assuming that the author's audience included women.

20. See David M. Carr and Colleen M. Conway, "The Divine-Human Marriage Matrix and Constructions of Gender and 'Bodies' in the Christian Bible," in *Sacred Marriages: The Divine-Human Sexual Metaphor from Sumer to Early Christianity*, ed. Martti Nissinen and Risto Uro (Winona Lake, IN: Eisenbrauns, 2008).

21. Edward W. Said, *Culture and Imperialism* (New York: Knopf, 1993), 149–50.

22. Lieu, *The Theology of the Johannine Epistles*, 36.

23. Ibid. Parsenios argues that "when Kipling says of East and West that never the twain shall meet, he is saying something that is both true and false for the function of the *sententiae* in the Johannine orbit." What is true is the irreconcilable difference between flesh/darkness and Spirit/light. What is different is that the Gospel's maxims "do not define the realms of darkness and light so sharply in order to signal that people are locked in one realm or the other, with no chance to change or choose, but rather, in order to emphasize the need to choose one over the other." *First, Second, and Third John*, 19.

24. Dube and Staley, "Descending from and Ascending into Heaven: A Postcolonial Analysis of Travel, Space and Power in John," 3.

Bibliography

Aland, Kurt, and Barbara Aland. *The Text of the New Testament: An Introduction to the Critical Editions and to the Theory and Practice of Modern Textual Criticism.* 2nd ed., rev. and enl. ed. Grand Rapids: Wm. B. Eerdmans, 1989.

Anderson, Paul N. *The Christology of the Fourth Gospel: Its Unity and Disunity in the Light of John 6.* Tübingen: Mohr, 1996.

Anderson, Paul N., Felix Just, and Tom Thatcher, eds. *John, Jesus, and History,* Society of Biblical Literature Symposium Series, vol. 44. Atlanta: Society of Biblical Literature, 2007.

Bauckham, Richard. *The Gospels for All Christians: Rethinking the Gospel Audiences.* Grand Rapids: Wm. B. Eerdmans, 1998.

Berlin, Adele. "Poetics and Interpretation of Biblical Narrative." Sheffield: Almond Press, 1983.

Borgen, Peder. "God's Agent in the Fourth Gospel." In *Religions in Antiquity. Essays in Memory of Erwin Ramsdell Goodenough,* edited by Jacob Neusner, 135–48. Leiden: E. J. Brill, 1968.

Bornkamm, Gunther. "Towards the Interpretation of the Fourth Gospel: A Discussion of *The Testament of Jesus* by Ernst Kasemann." In *The Interpretation of John,* edited by John Ashton, 97–119. Philadelphia; London: Fortress Press; SPCK, 1986.

Brant, Jo-Ann A. *Dialogue and Drama: Elements of Greek Tragedy in the Fourth Gospel.* Peabody, MA: Hendrickson Publishers, 2004.

Brown, Raymond E. *The Community of the Beloved Disciple.* New York: Paulist Press, 1979.

———. *The Gospel According to John (I–Xii).* The Anchor Bible. 1st ed. Garden City, NY: Doubleday, 1966.

173

———. "Roles of Women in the Fourth Gospel." *Theological Studies* 36 (1975): 688–99.

Bultmann, Rudolf. *The Gospel of John: A Commentary*. Philadelphia: Westminster Press, 1971.

Burridge, Richard A. *What Are the Gospels? A Comparison with Graeco-Roman Biography*. Grand Rapids: Eerdmans, 2004.

Carr, David M., and Colleen M. Conway. "The Divine-Human Marriage Matrix and Constructions of Gender and 'Bodies' in the Christian Bible." In *Sacred Marriages: The Divine-Human Sexual Metaphor from Sumer to Early Christianity*, edited by Martti Nissinen and Risto Uro, 275–303. Winona Lake, IN: Eisenbrauns, 2008.

Carter, Warren. *God in the New Testament*. Nashville: Abingdon Press, 2016.

———. *John and Empire: Initial Explorations*. New York: T & T Clark, 2008.

———. *Pontius Pilate: Portraits of a Roman Governor*. Collegeville, MN: Liturgical Press, 2003.

Claussen, Carsten. "John, Qumran, and the Question of Sectarianism." *Perspectives in Religious Studies* 37, no. 4 (2010): 421–40.

Coloe, Mary L. *God Dwells with Us: Temple Symbolism in the Fourth Gospel*. Collegeville, MN: Liturgical Press, 2001.

Coloe, Mary L., and Tom Thatcher, eds. *John, Qumran, and the Dead Sea Scrolls: Sixty Years of Discovery and Debate*. Atlanta: Society of Biblical Literature, 2011.

Conway, Colleen M. *Behold the Man: Jesus and Greco-Roman Masculinity*. Oxford; New York: Oxford University Press, 2008.

———. "'Behold the Man!' Masculine Christology and the Fourth Gospel." In *New Testament Masculinities*, edited by Stephen D. Moore and Janice Capel Anderson, 163–80. Atlanta: Society of Biblical Literature, 2003.

———. "Gender Matters in John." In *A Feminist Companion to John*, edited by Amy-Jill Levine, 79–103. Cleveland: Pilgrim, 2003.

———. *Men and Women in the Fourth Gospel: Gender and Johannine Characterization*. Atlanta: Society of Biblical Literature, 1999.

Cullmann, Oscar. *The Johannine Circle: Its Place in Judaism, among the Disciples of Jesus and in Early Christianity: A Study in the Origin of the Gospel of John*. New Testament Library. London: S.C.M. Press, 1976.

Culpepper, R. Alan. *Anatomy of the Fourth Gospel: A Study in Literary Design*. Philadelphia: Fortress Press, 1983.

———. *The Gospel and Letters of John*. Nashville: Abingdon Press, 1998.

———. *The Johannine School: An Evaluation of the Johannine-School Hypothesis Based on an Investigation of the Nature of Ancient Schools*. Missoula, MT: Scholars Press, 1975.

Dube, Musa W. "Reading for Decolonization (John 4:1-42)." In *John and Postcolonialism: Travel, Space and Power*, 51–75. London; New York: Sheffield, 2002.

Dube, Musa W., and Jeffrey L. Staley. "Descending from and Ascending into Heaven: A Postcolonial Analysis of Travel, Space and Power in John." In *John and Postcolonialism: Travel, Space and Power*, edited by Musa W. Dube and Jeffrey L. Staley, 1–10. London; New York: Sheffield, 2002.

Ford, J. Massyngberde. *Redeemer—Friend and Mother: Salvation in Antiquity and in the Gospel of John*. Minneapolis: Fortress Press, 1997.

Foxhall, Lin, and J. B. Salmon. *Thinking Men: Masculinity and Its Self-Representation in the Classical Tradition*. London; New York: Routledge, 1998.

———. *When Men Were Men: Masculinity, Power, and Identity in Classical Antiquity*. London; New York: Routledge, 1998.

Gandhi, Leela. *Postcolonial Theory: A Critical Introduction*. New York: Columbia University Press, 1998.

Gleason, Maud W. *Making Men: Sophists and Self-Presentation in Ancient Rome*. Princeton, NJ: Princeton University Press, 1995.

Hakola, Raimo. *Reconsidering Johannine Christianity: A Social Identity Approach*. New York: Routledge, Taylor & Francis Group, 2015.

Hiddleston, Jane. *Understanding Postcolonialism*. Stocksfield: Acumen, 2009.

Hill, Charles E. *The Johannine Corpus in the Early Church*. Oxford; New York: Oxford University Press, 2004.

Käsemann, Ernst. *The Testament of Jesus: A Study of the Gospel of John in the Light of Chapter 17*. London: S.C.M. Press, 1968.

Larsen, Kasper Bro, ed. *The Gospel of John as Genre Mosaic*. Göttingen; Bristol, CT: Vandenhoeck & Ruprecht, 2015.

———. *Recognizing the Stranger: Recognition Scenes in the Gospel of John*. Leiden; Boston: Brill, 2008.

Lee, Dorothy A. *Flesh and Glory: Symbol, Gender, and Theology in the Gospel of John*. New York: Crossroad, 2002.

Lieu, Judith. "The Audience of the Johannine Epistles." In *Communities in Dispute: Current Scholarship on the Johannine Epistles*, edited by R. Alan Culpepper and Paul N. Anderson, 123–40. Atlanta: SBL Press, 2014.

———. "Scripture and the Feminine in John." In *A Feminist Companion to the Hebrew Bible in the New Testament*, edited by Athalya Brenner, 225–40. Sheffield, England: Sheffield Academic Press, 1996.

———. *The Theology of the Johannine Epistles*. Cambridge; New York: Cambridge University Press, 1991.

Liew, Tat-siong Benny. "Queering Closets and Perverting Desires: Cross-Examining John's Engendering and Transgendering Word across Different Worlds." In *They Were All Together in One Place? Toward Minority Biblical Criticism*, edited by Randall C. Bailey, Tat-siong Benny Liew, and Fernando F. Segovia, 251–88. Leiden; Boston: Brill, 2009.

Loader, William. "Central Structure of Johannine Christology." *New Testament Studies* 30 (1984): 188–216.

———. *Jesus in John's Gospel: Structure and Issues in Johannine Christology*. Grand Rapids: Eerdmans, 2017.

Martyn, J. Louis. *History and Theology in the Fourth Gospel*. The New Testament Library. 3rd ed. Louisville, KY: Westminster John Knox Press, 2003.

Meeks, Wayne A. "The Man from Heaven in Johannine Sectarianism." *Journal of Biblical Literature* 91 (1972): 44–72.

Metzger, Bruce M. *The Text of the New Testament: Its Transmission, Corruption, and Restoration*, edited by Bart D. Ehrman. New York: Oxford University Press, 2005.

Moore, Stephen D. *Empire and Apocalpyse: Postcolonialism and the New Testament*. Sheffield: Sheffield Phoenix Press, 2006.

————. "Postcolonialism." In *Handbook of Postmodern Biblical Interpretation*, edited by A. K. M. Adam, 182–88. St. Louis, MO: Chalice Press, 2000.

Myers, Alicia D. "Gender, Rhetoric and Recognition: Characterizing Jesus and (Re)Defining Masculinity in the Gospel of John." *Journal for the Study of the New Testament* 38 (2015): 191–218.

Neyrey, Jerome H. *The Gospel of John in Cultural and Rhetorical Perspective*. Grand Rapids: Eerdmans, 2009.

————. "'My Lord and My God': The Divinity of Jesus in John's Gospel." *Society of Biblical Literature Seminar Papers* 25 (1986): 152–71.

Nongbri, Brent. "The Use and Abuse of P52: Papyrological Pitfalls in the Dating of the Fourth Gospel." *Harvard Theological Review* 98 (2005): 23–48.

O'Day, Gail R. "Gospel of John." In *Women's Bible Commentary*, edited by Carol A. Newsom, Sharon H. Ringe, and Jacqueline E. Lapsley, 517–30. Louisville, KY: Westminster John Knox, 2014.

O'Grady, John F. "The Human Jesus in the Fourth Gospel." *Biblical Theology Bulletin* 14 (1984): 63–66.

Painter, John, and Daniel J. Harrington. *1, 2, and 3 John*. Collegeville, MN: Liturgical Press, 2002.

Parsenios, George L. *Departure and Consolation: The Johannine Farewell Discourses in Light of Greco-Roman Literature*. Leiden; Boston: Brill, 2005.

————. *First, Second, and Third John*. Grand Rapids: Baker Academic, 2014.

Perkins, Pheme. *The Johannine Epistles*. Wilmington, DE: Michael Glazier, 1979.

————. "The Relationship Between the Gospel and 1 John." In *Commu-*

nities in Dispute: Current Scholarship on the Johannine Epistles, edited by R. Alan Culpepper and Paul N. Anderson, 95–122. Atlanta: SBL Press, 2014.

Reinhartz, Adele. "The Johannine Community and Its Jewish Neighbors: A Reappraisal." In *What Is John? Vol. 2, Literary and Social Readings of the Fourth Gospel*, edited by Fernando F. Segovia, 111–39. Atlanta: Scholars Press, 1998.

————. *The Word in the World: The Cosmological Tale in the Fourth Gospel.* Atlanta: Scholars Press, 1992.

Ringe, Sharon H. *Wisdom's Friends: Community and Christology in the Fourth Gospel.* 1st ed. Louisville, KY: Westminster John Knox Press, 1999.

Said, Edward W. *Culture and Imperialism.* 1st ed. New York: Knopf, 1993.

Schneiders, Sandra M. "Women in the Fourth Gospel and the Role of Women in the Contemporary Church." *Biblical Theology Bulletin* 12 (1982): 35–45.

Schnelle, Udo. *Antidocetic Christology in the Gospel of John: An Investigation of the Place of the Fourth Gospel in the Johannine School.* Minneapolis: Fortress Press, 1992.

Schüssler Fiorenza, Elisabeth. *Jesus: Miriam's Child, Sophia's Prophet: Critical Issues in Feminist Christology.* New York: Continuum, 1994.

Scott, Martin. *Sophia and the Johannine Jesus.* Sheffield: Sheffield Academic Press, 1992.

Segovia, Fernando F. "The Gospel of John." In *A Postcolonial Commentary on the New Testament Writings*, edited by Fernando F. Segovia and R. S. Sugirtharajah, 156–93. London: T & T Clark, 2009.

————. "The Journey(s) of the Word of God: A Reading of the Plot of the Fourth Gospel." *Semeia* 53 (1991): 23–54.

Seim, Turid Karlsen. "Descent and Divine Paternity in the Gospel of John: Does the Mother Matter?" *New Testament Studies* 51 (2005): 361–75.

————. "Motherhood and the Making of Fathers in Antiquity: Contextualizing Genetics in the Gospel of John." In *Women and Gender in*

Ancient Religions: Interdisciplinary Approaches, edited by Paul A. Holloway, Stephen P. Ahearne-Kroll, and James A. Kelhoffer, 99–123. Tubingen: Mohr Siebeck, 2010.

Sissa, Giulia. *The Daily Life of the Greek Gods*. Stanford, CA: Stanford University Press, 2000.

Stibbe, Mark W. G. *The Gospel of John as Literature: An Anthology of Twentieth-Century Perspectives*. Leiden; New York: E.J. Brill, 1993.

———. *John as Storyteller: Narrative Criticism and the Fourth Gospel*. Cambridge; New York: Cambridge University Press, 1992.

Stovell, Beth M. *Mapping Metaphorical Discourse in the Fourth Gospel: John's Eternal King*. Linguistic Biblical Studies. Leiden; Boston: Brill, 2012.

Sugirtharajah, R. S., ed. *The Postcolonial Biblical Reader*. Malden, MA: Blackwell, 2006.

Thatcher, Tom. *Greater Than Caesar: Christology and Empire in the Fourth Gospel*. Minneapolis: Fortress Press, 2009.

———. *Why John Wrote a Gospel: Jesus—Memory—History*. Louisville, KY: Westminster John Knox Press, 2006.

Thompson, Marianne Meye. *The Humanity of Jesus in the Fourth Gospel*. Philadelphia: Fortress Press, 1988.

Um, Stephen T. *The Theme of Temple Christology in John's Gospel*. London; New York: T & T Clark, 2006.

Williams, Craig A. *Roman Homosexuality: Ideologies of Masculinity in Classical Antiquity*. Oxford; New York: Oxford University Press, 1999; rev. ed., 2010.

Zanker, Paul. "The Power of Images in the Age of Augustus." Ann Arbor: University of Michigan Press, 1990. Aland, Kurt, and Barbara Aland. *The Text of the New Testament: An Introduction to the Critical Editions and to the Theory and Practice of Modern Textual Criticism*. Grand Rapids: W.B. Eerdmans, 1989.

Scripture Index

Hebrew Bible

Second Temple Literature

New Testament